IN THE EARLY WORLD

IN THE EARLY WORLD

EARLY WORLD

ELWYN S. RICHARDSON

The blue heron stands in the early world,
Looking like a freezing blue cloud in the morning.
                                        —Irene

PANTHEON BOOKS

A DIVISION OF RANDOM HOUSE

NEW YORK

FIRST AMERICAN EDITION

Library of Congress Catalog Card Number: 75-79800

Manufactured in the United States of America

FOREWORD

THERE are few things certain about compulsory schooling, but two of the most important are that it is the greatest adventure mankind has yet undertaken and that so far it is only in the uncertain beginnings of what will be a long evolution. To its evolution, it is not too much to claim, this book makes a significant contribution. Uneven, often almost wilful in its approach, it gives nevertheless a vivid picture of a school full of vitality in pursuit of values deeply rooted in the children's lives and capable of serving them lifelong. Oruaiti School functioned as a community of artists and scientists who turned a frank and searching gaze on all that came within their ambit. Curiosity and emotional force led them to explore together the natural world and the world of their feelings. They learned to esteem each other's explorations, discoveries, and records with tact and with discriminating enthusiasm, so that a fine collective strength was developed. a strength depending on each child making an individual search and bringing to the group what only he could give. In return the group sustained each child and valued his discoveries; its achievements pressed him on to further exploration. This feeling grew from the direction of the common search and the wholeness it gave the children.

In this school too there was a proper recognition of the making propensity. Homo faber and homo ludens were together in the child who thought and felt. Studies and activities grew naturally out of what preceded them. New techniques were discovered and skills practised as each achievement set new standards. In such an 'integrated' curriculum the integrity of persons is preserved even more than the integrity of topics. Children recognize themselves in and through the things they make. From their paintings, their prints and their pottery they learn answers to the question 'Who am I?' They are then free to respect others for their achievements and their insight because they themselves, standing amid the work of their hands, take a solid pride in their own craftsmanship or artistry.

In much discussion of teaching there is an assumption that a radical difference of kind exists between work

v

which is variously called 'creative', 'imaginative', or 'expressive'—work which is about children's feelings and sensations—and, on the other hand, work which is distinguished as 'factual' and which concerns the 'real' or 'outside' world. Attitudes that follow from this assumption induce children to write 'creatively' by injecting an artificial heightening of tone or a spurious fancy into an otherwise straightforward account, and force them into a clipped, inelegantly dull jargon whenever presenting a report. It seems evident from the work at Oruaiti that the distinction has little relevance to the work of children. A matter-of-fact acceptance of a total event in which feelings are involved with all the other facts of the situation permits a growth in awareness and a search for exactness which the usual view prevents or hinders. These children turned the same dispassionate and unselfconscious regard on to their own feelings as on to other events, and pursued with the same relentless demand for exactitude a fact of natural science or a fact of human response. It is this that made possible the beauty of the poetry, the excellence of the graphic and ceramic work, and the careful scientific observation. Because the children were not required to make a divorce between the parts of their experience, a divorce hostile to their intuitive grasp of situations, they could bend to their work with an enthusiasm and a degree of concentration which ordinary schooling never touches.

And always the school functioned as a community, a community of artist-scientists. In considering the work so amply laid out here we must pay attention to both elements, the community and the individual artist-scientists. The school functioned as a community not in spite of but because of the individualism of its members—each person counted and was expected to make his own contribution to its life. Personal views, even eccentric ones, were welcomed. The primary demand on the child was that he should think through to exactly what he observed, felt, or believed. As is made clear in the course of the book a great deal of careful training went into eliminating the merely stock response and the expected answer. But combined with this demand for the expression of a personal view, and of course necessary to it, was the willing acceptance of idiosyncrasy and the affectionate acceptance of the strengths and limitations of each member of the group. In this school this was made possible by mutual recognition of artistic achievement.

T. S. Eliot remarks that the experience of enjoying a bad work of art is qualitatively different from that of enjoying a good work of art. The former mis-educates just as surely as the latter educates. This is especially true of the child's own work. To be appreciated and to value oneself on account of sentimental or spurious work is to dry up the springs of genuine emotion. One of the most important objects of study in the work of Oruaiti, therefore, is to see how aesthetic standards were established and maintained. The children were not chosen in any way. Many of them came from homes from which the radio, the gramophone, and magazines were excluded; they seldom met with other families except for religious purposes; they saw no films, and often the only reading in the household was biblical. Other families were gregarious, and the children were influenced by radio, films, and so on, as far as these were available in a small rural community. The influence of books was small. In this account we can trace step by step the children's increasing awareness of the world around them and their increasing desire to express its subtleties adequately and vividly, going hand in hand with the glad recognition of high achievement in the expression of others. The means by which valid artistic statement was established as the principal value round which the life of the school grew is the most fascinating of the main threads running through this book. The process was a delicate one, with the teacher leading and directing but at the same time humbly ready to learn from the children. All of them, children and teacher, pursued the one end, which was to realise precisely and to express adequately their growing awareness of the world around them. This kind of school grew out of the nature of this teacher with these children. It was a long slow process, in which humble beginnings made a foundation for later and better expression and where each new achievement was made a springboard for later leaps in imagination and understanding.

One often hears the view that in education through the arts the end product does not matter—that it is only the process which matters. But this is unduly simple-minded. Unless the work is freshly conceived, formally satisfying, and expresses a personal attitude, the making is repetitive and routine rather than a search into the nature of the thing and the nature of the self. Children will grow and develop fully in imaginative and aesthetic insight only in a classroom where high standards prevail and where their work will be tested by the critical insight of others, so that both its strength and its weakness are revealed. Only then are they stimulated to live in the fullness of their powers. In the beginning the pressure towards awareness and discrimination comes from the teacher. But since if it comes only from the teacher or if it remains mainly with the teacher the pressure will produce only imitative performance, the weight of feeling must become a community one as quickly as possible. The means by which this was done at Oruaiti are clearly demonstrated throughout the book. An essential part was the non-directive discussion which took place so often and was a continuous background to all the work of the class. The loving care which caused every child to be treated as a person in his own right and gave the teacher his sincere interest in the response each child made to his environment was communicated to the children. This sharing was extended as work in the arts revealed always more fully to each child the insights and feelings of the others. In this way love and understanding grew together, providing the only medium in which work with this quality could grow.

How much the children understand of the symbolism an adult can detect in their work is a moot question and probably unanswerable, but there is no doubt that the moods so sensitively conveyed by many poems, and so clearly understood by other children who comment on them, are 'intended' in the sense that they were recognized when the idea took verbal form and that they were the reason for the child to write it down. Thus the poem *This Morning* on page 94 conveys a melancholy which clearly was recognized by David H. when he wrote. But the phrase 'hollow as trumpets' in *The River,* page 94, which has so many overtones for an adult ear seems to be a simple visual parallel. But who can doubt that, for children as for adults, the resonances of such a phrase reach down through many levels of consciousness to awaken and drag towards explicit realization what stirs only dimly. Whatever the degree and kind of their symbolism it is quite certain that these children were enabled by their poetry, their prints, their masks, and their painting to recognize aspects of themselves and to accept them in ways that would have been impossible otherwise. These embodiments of past selves provided a record for the individual and for his fellows which placed both their care for each other and their self-respect on a sure foundation.

Possibly it was the search for just such a foundation which led Elwyn Richardson to embark on the eight-year experiment recorded here, to persist with it in the teeth of all kinds of difficulties and hazards, and finally to incur the labour of compiling this record.

The school at Oruaiti consisted of a square wooden room built in 1889, roofed with red-painted corrugated iron, gable-ended, weather-boarded, and with three high double-hung windows on each of its sides. Behind this building and a little to one side was a grey pre-fab which formed the senior classroom. To go into this room, even without the children, was to be dazzled by a riot of colours, shapes, and textures. Drums, pots, mobiles dangling from the ceiling, masks, painting, printing gear, a small electric kiln—all the disorder of a dozen simultaneous workshops was pent up in this small room. But there was discernible a pattern, or perhaps a series of patterns, the kind of pattern which children can feel at home in, where the organization is sometimes the minimal amount necessary for efficient working and sometimes the exaggerated arranging lavished on a sacred object or a sacred process. It was a room of shrines cohabitating with the muddle which is incidental to utter absorption in a task, a room through long experience immediately submissive to every change of mood imposed upon it by its masters.

When Elwyn Richardson went to Oruaiti this lay in the future. Then, there was only one building, a small paved yard terminated by a grove of trees, grass and sheds leading away to banks sloping down into a swamp on one side and up to the hill on the other. The main road lay behind and a clay access road ran slantwise up the bank by the swamp to the school gate. Tall grass, gorse, and bracken dominated the open area, willows and manuka, the river bank and flats beyond the road. In some respects he was taking refuge in Oruaiti, but he came as well because of an interest in molluscs which Northland would allow him to pursue. Apart from a certain rebelliousness and a desire to justify himself there was little to suggest his future development as a teacher. He had begun to train as a scientist, obviously he had excellent aesthetic taste, and his previous experience had led him to resent control and to sympathize with those who felt as he did. He was capable of giving respect and affection to children and needed to feel that he had earned theirs in return. Together with a number of fortuities these characteristics shaped his approach to teaching and, over the first few years, started him along that path of free democratic consultation and of expression through the arts which was to permeate and transform what began as a rather formal stance and a predominantly scientific outlook.

In a sense therefore Oruaiti is unique. But it is unique in the sense that the children's work shown in these pages is unique. Every piece illustrated grew out of an individual history, out of an encounter with the materials of an art, and out of confident self-acceptance. In the school as a whole, too, teaching expressed Elwyn Richardson's nature by giving children the opportunity to reach their full height as artists, as craftsmen, as scientists, and as students, through the establishment of a community where self-respect demanded this generosity in giving and receiving. In this sense every classroom can uniquely express its own mode of co-operative individualism. As teaching becomes more conscious an art the journeyman will move closer to the satisfactions of this kind of teaching, and new generations of children will learn to recognize and understand the value of work into which love has flowed.

JOHN MELSER

CONTENTS

Fern design, Raymond, 10 years

To the children of Oruaiti, who made this work
possible; and to their parents, who accepted my
methods and discoveries as the normal way of
educational growth.

E.S.R.

INTRODUCTION

THIS book is about my attempts to understand children, especially their ability and desire to express themselves in their own natural ways. My attempts began with crafts, and these drew my attention to the individual idiom of each child in art, in music, in movement, in drama, and ultimately in language.

After a time Eunice Foster came and worked with me for two years. She helped especially with the development of art and crafts in the infant room, and then with drama and writing. Her children did outstanding work with fabric and lino printing. Later Cherry Raymond came, and in her time we learned to understand much about the individual idiom that each child can develop in language when encouraged.

In this work the children themselves made many discoveries of technique and of appreciation. We learned from them as we went along. Comparatively little professional writing on creative education came my way during these years, and I began with only sketchy educational beliefs; but I now realise that what I have learned from my children and recorded here supports some well established educational beliefs. For what I myself learned during these years I have mainly my children to thank. They were my teachers as I was theirs, and the basis of our relationship was sincerity, without which, I am convinced, there can be no creative education.

ELWYN S. RICHARDSON

Auckland
September 1964

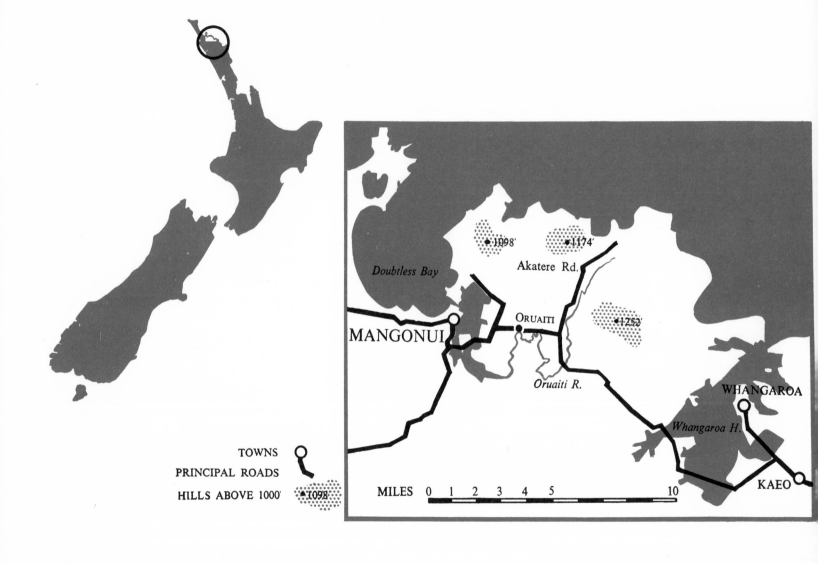

TOWNS

PRINCIPAL ROADS

HILLS ABOVE 1000' ▲1098'

MANGONUI

Doubtless Bay

1098'

1174'

Akatere Rd.

Oruaiti

1252'

Oruaiti R.

WHANGAROA

Whangaroa H.

KAEO

MILES 0 1 2 3 4 5   10

IN THE EARLY WORLD

Oruaiti School

1

THE SCHOOL

BEFORE all the others Dennis was there, sitting on the seat in the playground, looking forlorn, perhaps annoyed. The emotion was hard to place. What could have persuaded him to arrive at eight o'clock? Even his mother was mystified.

'Why is it,' she asked, 'that just when I don't expect it young Dennis must be off to school at this early hour?' Whatever the cause, Dennis was there, and not very pleased, evidently. The frown upon his face, usually so open and smiling below his mop of unruly light coloured hair, suggested disappointment. Something just hadn't happened that he had wanted to happen.

He had already walked in all the puddles and had a swing on the long rope over the clay slide. His bare legs and battered striped jersey gave evidence of that. He hadn't enjoyed it much. He had also found the large tractor tyre in the bracken, where Ted had hidden it for himself the night before. It and his two driving sticks, which only Raymond would dare to borrow, lay propped on the seat beside him. He looked down the road again to Valerie's place. So it must have been Clifton or Eric or Ted that he was expecting; for only they, besides the girls (and Dennis wouldn't be waiting for them), lived at the end of the valley. It could have been Sonny though, if he came with his father on the tractor.

Dennis watched the dripping tap at the nearby tank-stand. 'I could water the clay slide,' he thought, 'and the steep hill where Clif got stuck with his truck yesterday. But what's the use?'

He heard footsteps coming up the gravelled drive and jumped up, and finding words springing to his lips even as he saw it was his school teacher, Miss F., approaching with her bag of books.

'Eric . . . Oh! It's you, Miss F. I thought it might be Eric. He promised to come early, so that we could build our roads for the tyres. But he hasn't turned up!'

It was Eric then, who had let him down. Well, no wonder! For Eric, besides having to help milk the cows, has his bantams to feed every morning, unless one of his sisters, Jennifer or Necia, would do it for him. Then there was a tramp of two long miles across the paddocks

1

of Clifton's and Valerie's farms. That is if he missed the cream truck. It was more usual however to see Eric arrive with Ronny, Lawrence, and the girls, clutching cream-cans on the slippery back of the truck.

Miss F., friend to all the little people, stopped in front of Dennis, fumbling for her keys in her satchel.

'It's very early, Dennis,' she said. 'I'm especially early because I want to duplicate some of those story books for the primers to read. Like to turn the handle?'

'Oh heck, Miss F.! I wanna play,' said our Dennis.

Miss F. had walked two miles from her home at the head of the valley, where she lives with her mother and her father, now a retired farmer. So she has just about as far to go as Eric. But then her road is the main highway that fringes the northern side of the valley, far easier under foot than the 'cow plod holes', of which Valerie speaks, that cover the wet flats about the river. Just over the way from her home is Dennis's home, where now brother David is probably getting out of bed to help with the end of the milking, which his two other brothers, Kelvin and Bevin, started at six o'clock.

'I suppose David is still in bed, if I know him,' continued Dennis. 'Did you see him, Miss F.?'

'He was out feeding your hens and turkeys, when I came past. By the way, your mother asked me to tell you that you'd better remember her words to you of last night, if coming to school early has anything to do with getting your clothes so dirty. Those you took off yesterday evening were mud all over.'

Miss F. didn't seem to enjoy passing on that message, for Dennis only looked unhappier. She is a kindly person with a love for all children, and the suggestion of a willow stick waiting at home for Dennis was too much to repeat. It is so long since she had to concern herself with punishment that she avoids the thought of it. Dennis was so dirty, he should consider his mother though.

'Eric won't arrive at this hour,' she said. 'Anyway here's Walter and his sister Kathleen coming.'

'I've been waiten and waiten, Miss F.,' moaned young Dennis, who had forgotten to speak in the more correct manner that he reserved for teachers and grown-ups.

'When he said he would come, he should have.' A reflective pause and a heavier stamp in the muddied puddle by the seat. 'And David will be getting all the turns on the tractor as well.'

But Walter, alias Wattie, disrupted these complaints and though Eric had been the confidant of yesterday, it appeared that Wattie was threatening that position today. In a few minutes the tyres were bowling their way over roads and bridges, up on to planks and down again, then racing across the playground.

The handle of the duplicator turned on, the tyres moved on, and the clock crept on. Others arrived. Rosalie and sister Lorna came over the paddock from their home, next door to the school.

'Get the tennis bats and the ball,' said Lorna.

'Get me one too,' called Mavis when she saw Rosalie going into Miss F.'s room.

'And me too,' said Kathleen.

The four girls were soon absorbed in their game. To the pat of the ball upon the court and the batting over the net, a tune was singing in Rosalie's head:

> My sister Lorna
> She sits in the corner,
> Singing 'Little Baby Jesus'
> All by herself.

'Yous fellas go play ping-pong somewhere else!' shouted Wattie as the tyres came along the pink lines of the courts, which really are 'roads' and not part of the game court, or that's what Walter thought. What's a sister if you can't tell her what you think, anyway?

The other tyres had now found drivers, and Kenneth had arrived with his little brother, Maurice, who is too small to manage a tyre for more than a few minutes. Sonny had come on the tractor after all with his father, who was on his way to work for Rosalie's father.

Clifton had drifted in timidly, as is his way, and if his engine roared loudly and with confidence his orders to Ken and Sonny were faltering and without force. He is a very shy little boy of whom Mary said, 'He is like a mouse who is just too scared to go into the middle of the room.' This does not mean that he is unprepared to express himself or to make himself felt. He has had several fights with Brett, who thought that force of arm could take a tyre from him. A wordy fellow, this Brett! His father had just dropped him off with his younger

Tyre games

brother David. He'll be airing his opinions somewhere with Allan and Ronny.

The cream truck had now arrived. Necia and Jennifer jumped down from it and ran up the clay bank through the fence, the shortest way to their classroom, before joining Mavis and the three others with the bats. Eric slid off the back, yelled 'Thank you Fred!' and walked slowly up the road, the long way, to the play-

3

ground. With hands in outsize pockets, with a rip in the seat of trousers that surely must have belonged to brother Ronny at some time, he walked on bare feet across sore stones and stopped to watch the line of truck and bus drivers tearing past him.

'I had to help milk this morning,' he shouted to Dennis who was passing by.

'I said, I had to help Dad. . . Did you hear me Dennis?' Ken came roaring slowly by, obviously in crawler low gear, and Dennis ran off the road to Eric.

'Sorry, Eric, I'm busy. I'm an articulator with a load of tyres for Kaitaia, and I . . . The rest was lost as Sonny zoomed past on the last lap to Kaitaia, and Eric sat down on the playground seat. He was looking and feeling glum. No tyres left, of course!

'Can I borrow your tyre, Ken?'

'Finished with your tyre, Sonny?'

Well, he had better go across and hobnob with the other older boys who usually gather on the steps or in one of the classrooms to talk over the happenings of the last weekend or the news of the three communities that are represented at the school. Ronny was the sage of these discussions. In a very adult way he directed the conversations on matters of hawks and hens, sheep and dog, pheasants and dogs.

'Waiaua people not here yet?' asked Brett. The people from Akatere, an almost intermontane basin at the northern end of the valley, had arrived by school bus at eight twenty. Walter and Kathleen, Martha, Mary and Mike were some of these people, and David the eldest. There are three Davids at the school. There is Brett's young brother, a tough little collar-around-the-ankles boy of eight. Then there is David W. He's sometimes given an alias by the boys; they call him 'Tiger'. The last David is thirteen, a lithe-limbed strong boy full of energy with a comment for every situation in the day's work.

The little people were by now patterned about the grounds: on the swing, a single rope Maori type swing, under the bluegums, by the old kiln, on the games courts in groups talking, and in lines driving tyres. Unorganized, but full of the organization which is so important to children's social growth.

Akatere is over the hill, and there feeling is loyal to the community of the coast with its sheltered bays and sea-fringed cottages rather than to the valley community. Then too there is the strong valley bond of religion. For all but one family are of Brethren faith, whereas the Akatere Maori farmers have their link with the nearby Convent, where at some time of their lives, all these children attend, David, Mary, Kathleen and the others.

Ronny and the boys were talking about the sheep and cattle-drafting they had helped with at the last weekend. Ronny had helped Allan's and Rosalie's fathers muster at the open coast itself, where most of the Brethren farmers have runs.

'All these farms were once Maori lands,' said David H., 'but my grandfather sold most of his share so we could farm our home farm better. That's how we got our cows and the fifty acres of grass and the small house too.

The little trickle of a creek that gathers in the lower region of these hills of Akatere, flows away south from the farms and homes of Barbara and her streamside garden, Kathleen and her duck pens and chicken huts, Sarah and her apple tree, to meet the Oruaiti River at the head of the valley. It passes Dennis's and David W.'s home, then winds across the fertile floodplain to the foot of the track leading up to the school, and so on to the lower, slower saltings and swamps of the upper Mangonui Harbour.

This stream is part of every child's experience. Ever growing, it passes through the pools where David's pet eels live, below the old willows where Clifton and Valerie go to see the shags return to roost at night, by the bank where Jennifer's pukekos stalk to the region of the river. Here where the tidal flux is felt, Ted and Nell fish for snapper and catch eels. It is of such things that Ronny and Allan might have been talking when Eric joined them.

The small blue bus had yet to arrive from the other direction, where this broad muddy river spills out over the upper harbour and mudflats. Here, small fringing farms climb up from its shores into the hills of fern, tall scrub and gorse, and here and there are the few remaining patches of native bush, so like the country that rings in the Oruaiti valley itself. From creamstand to cream-stand the blue bus noses along the clay-drowned metal road to the beach, where Sonny, Irene, Mary, Eliza, Snowy, and John live. From these sands they trail sponges and seaweeds crusted with corals and mussels bearded with hydroids, and sea-worn sticks bristled with goose barnacles, and in their pockets are the gathered glory of the high-tide line, pebbles with beautiful markings, shells in all shapes and colours, glints of the lovely paua shell, and shaped pieces of kina, the green sea-egg. In the sandhills they see the oyster-catcher running to lead them away from its nest, and behind in the taro-covered swamps the bitterns walking statuesquely among the algae, rushes, and sedges.

The bus arrived at school to find the scene unchanged: still the articulators, the games girls, the groups of boys talking.

'I could do with some free time for my story this morning. What do you chaps think?' asked Ronny.

Brett saw his cue. 'I want to write up the results of our experimental work on rocket development.'

'What experimental work?' asked someone.

'I and David are inventing a rocket at home. We have a prototype all ready for fueling tonight.'

'What's a proto-what?' asked Eric.

'First one, Eric,' said Brett. 'No one ever made one like ours.'

'I'll bet,' said Allan.

'Dad told you to keep quiet about our rocket, Brett,' said David.

5

'Well I'm not divulging much information really. I'll write up full plans for its development, but I will mark the folio "Not for Magazine". That means Sir can read it, but no others.'

A pause, in which he reflected on the subject, and then before David could start talking about his motor-bike 'bitzer', he went on, 'I don't see why I should have to keep quiet about it anyway. What's wrong with a few match heads? Now if we had a bit of liquid oxygen . . . . Some day I'll go into orbit.'

'And they'll lock you up,' said Allan.

'I've got a beaut idea for a large lino-cut for my poem. It's a horse-story one.'

'I think we should have some more time to work out things we can do with tyres. There aren't enough of them anyway.'

'It's really good fun getting over the course without falling over.'

'We plan to let it off on the mudflat in front of home, when the weather is perfect. We've got a length of cracker fuse that will make it safe for all personnel. The blast will be terrific, I hope.'

'Dennis says he got here at eight and you didn't come Eric.'

'Too bad! Too bad! Too bad!'

The girls on the other hand have little propensity for talking about such things. Several of them were in with Miss F. helping with the end of the duplicating.

'Anna's gone to the city, Miss F. She's gone to work now 'cause school's finished for her,' said Martha.

'Did you know that that man Ralph, the Maori man, is a relation of mine, Miss F.?'

'Yes, he is, 'cause he's going out with my big sister.'

'He paints pictures. Freda calls him an artist.'

'My little sister is coming to school soon.'

Yes, the girls are more interested in people, than in the things of the farm that the boys talk about so much.

The clock has gone round. All the children from Oruaiti, where the school is situated, have arrived, even Valerie. Time was allowed for the swapping of a few experiences, and then the bell rang. The groups of boys walked to their classrooms, while Mavis had a last hit over the net, a stroke full of imitative style but not skill. The ball soared up into the air over the wattles and into the bracken. She ran to look for it, joined by Kathleen.

'Tell Sir we are looking for a ball and will be in very soon,' shouted Kathleen, looming large in the fern.

Even before the bell rang there were many children in the classrooms. Some had come in talking; one or two were looking for things and sorting papers; Brett was reading; and Jennifer was smoothing off a twenty-inch clay mask that she had just taken from a plaster mould, preparatory to ornamenting it with ochre clips and iron sands. Valerie was peering in the new book in which she did all of her school work; it was neat and orderly—for her; it gave her pleasure just to be able to look at it and reflect upon the good beginning, though things were bound to get out of hand later, for Valerie was rather an untidy girl.

'I don't think you saw my story that I wrote yesterday. Anyway there's no mark on it anywhere,' said Valerie.

Slowly, without ceremony, the children entered, with Mavis a good last. Jennifer continued her mask, Brett's head remained in his book. But they and the others who had things unfinished knew that soon all would discuss the day's work and, if there was any point in it, make a brief assessment of work of the previous day.

'You wanna keep your head outa my things, Christopher,' whispered Dennis. 'Pity Christopher is such a big boy and so strong,' he thought, 'or I'd have . . . . Well, he's not such a bad chap really . . . Big though!'

The day had begun, and Brett became conscious of the silence as we began to organize those elements that were to be taught that morning. Jennifer smoothed her index finger around and around the large eyes of the wet clay mask, looking away, smoothing, listening. It was a one-room committee meeting, yet more homely, in that anyone was free to raise any subject he wished, as a sort of continuation of the playground discussions. We spoke as friends interested, without any formality, in a manner which had grown up with us. Perhaps our subject would be the answer to some question. 'What really would happen to us if the level of fall-out reached the point of danger to our health?' 'Tell us something about that hard-case chap who wrote the poem about Tam?' 'After Godliness and cleanliness, don't you think that punctuality should come about there?' Dennis had asked that last question.

'And rats to you, Dennis!' said someone.

Some listen and say nothing; yet isn't listening itself in a way a reply? Perhaps the only person who always has something to say is Brett. These discussion periods are, as often as not, a time when a considerable amount of information has to be imparted. The subject is always something about which the children are very interested, for the suggestions if they do come are from the children. Sometimes they are about things they have heard their parents discussing from the daily paper or the nearby township. The topics are usually most valuable ones and when the occasion arises questions and comments can go on for half an hour or so. This does not happen every day, nor is it necessary on every day to write up the series of lessons that they plan. Some days organize themselves. There are always a few children, too, who have a well filled day planned from many of their own interests. Yet on this day someone on the fringe of the discussion pulled out his books and started the formal sums set for that day. He wasn't interested in the subject of discussion. Perhaps he couldn't quite follow it. Eric sighed when it was all over, and Brett went on explaining to David, alias 'Tiger', who hadn't got the message.

'Leave my pencils alone in future Christopher, or you'll get your nose burnt by the rays,' was Dennis's comment after the discussion on radioactivity.

'Could we talk about African pygmies again this week?' asked Necia. 'Dad was telling us that he saw one once in a circus, and although he was only the size of Christopher or Ronny . . .'

'Not as big as me?' commented Allan.

'And he looked as old as Dad,' went on Necia.

'Heck, as old as that!' said Eric, who like most of the children thought Dad was very old.

'That's what she said,' said Allan.

Pleasantly ticked the clock, but discussion time was over; a number of the topics of the playground had been brought into the school; suggestions had been made about writing some interesting pieces for the magazine; some paintings had been suggested.

'A poem about the dew on the grass would be good,' said Mavis. The suggestions had been helpful on the whole, except, as Necia thought, 'Allan isn't very much use to me.' A number of these suggestions would be worked on later in the morning when there was to be a time for individual work. Many then started on the lessons for the day; formal sums occupied a part of each child's time. The nine-year-olds were making up problems involving subtraction.

'Here's mine, you jokers,' said Wattie. 'If I had four hundred and twenty-nine sea eggs and we ate two hundred and eighty-seven at dinner, what did we have left?'

'Good one, Wattie! How many did you eat yourself?' asked Ken.

'Oh, I ate the most,' added Walter.

Sums were checked in pairs, but even then there were errors and these had to be discussed at once.

The upper form children were reading over written work presented for the magazine, while the number work went on. One part of the group was listening to the sense of the readings while the other watched to see errors as the sentences unfolded themselves.

'Good sentence that one, but I think those two words may be wrong: disappoint and realation.'

'No, disappoint is all right, but the other's wrong. Irene will have to look it up,' said the reader, Mavis.

'Come off it,' said Brett, 'you should know it has no 'a'. Relation is r-e-l-a-t-i-o-n.'

'On the whole, I think that it is a very well written story, and it's interesting enough,' was one of David's comments.

'I agree with that,' went on Martha, 'and I think we should give the story a mark of three.'

'Three's only all right for the magazine, so you don't think it is such a good story, eh Martha?' said the chairman.

In this way stories were discussed by the group. A certain amount of individual work had been going on during the morning too. Jennifer had finished her mask, decorated with red ochre slips and iron-sand.

'Come and have a look at this mask,' said Mary, and a few came and stood around admiring it. Eric was one, because he is rather inclined to want to get away from his work.

The Maori swing

'Lovely big eyes! I like the rings around them. They stick out like fat bottles.'

'Put a bit here, Jenny. It doesn't look filled up enough just there.' She pointed to the sides of the chin. 'Put a hole in it. That would be good.'

'I would like to make a mask in your mould, Jennifer,' said David. 'Clear the deck for me, you jokers. I'll show you how the H——s work.' Soon David was at work, full of the inspiration given him by Jennifer's work.

Another group went on with a discussion on words that end in 'ment'. Lists were shown, and attempts were made to find a general principle that would help with words of that kind.

'I see the dictionary says "judgement" is correct and that "judgment" is too; that's kind of them,' said Owen.

'It generally appears that the "e" remains. That's as far as I would go,' was Irene's comment.

'I say always, except for one word I have found that doesn't, that's "argument".'

'Your rule falls to bits on Owen's words,' said Valerie, who had a very good knowledge of language. The discussion proceeded, for one section was loth to make generalizations and the other wanted them, but along the way good work was done in making the children more conscious of words. That was the point of the lesson.

The play bell rang, and a number pushed aside their work and went to the playgrounds. A few carried on for a time, but then the shouts outside sounded too enticing and in a few moments the room was deserted.

Allan's sums lay open where he had left them; Mary's story she had been working on for the past half-hour was open; David's big mask mould was half filled; Martha's work-book was open at the last page, where she had been filling in a list of errors she had been making in English grammar—perhaps after play she would work out some exercises on these errors for a few minutes; Glenis's and Owen's desks were covered with pieces of paper on which were the parts of poems that they had written that morning—glue-pot and scissors were evidence of their attempts to arrange their two poems in a way that satisfied them most. The pieces of the poem lay under rulers and pencils ready for glue-ing to a plain sheet of paper; some of it looked 'finished' and ready to paste.

FISH

The washed bones of fish
Lie rotting,
Rotting . . . .
Away, away
Cleaned by the birds at hand
The ever roaring sea shone them
The ever roaring sea shone them
The sun-baked head
With a hole for an eye
Looking nowhere

A wind came from the open doorway and several papers spiralled to the floor; they remained there, for the room was empty.

After the recess, further play with the tyres was asked for, just to see if more things could be worked out. The children had found out how to bowl them in an unusual way with two sticks, also in pairs with a stick each, and on this day attempts were made to jump tyres over obstacles. A new sport had been developed: tyre-jumping over piles of bricks.

'If you like to bowl one slowly, jump over me,' said Dennis to Raymond lying down on the concrete.

Relays with tyres followed, and then a game. Clifton, who is a very small boy sat out of the game and watched.

'Where's Brett?'

'Readen,' said Wattie.

The game went on, and at the end there was pure movement for its own sake; there was moving for fun and interpretative movement: blown by the wind as a leaf, then as a bird up into the sky; as a paper bag and a newspaper, because there had been a poem read to them the day before about a newspaper blown in a street. There were a few imaginative things like jumping into clouds, being blown away, then raining on mountains. Being ice age bears was probably best fun for Owen and Eric. Lastly a few fantastic things, such as landing on Mars, for the benefit of Brett who had just joined the class.

'I know a bit about this, you chaps. Careful! Move slowly there, Mary, 'cause the gravity is different. I can jump twelve feet in the air. Watch!' he said.

Others who had only heard of Mars gathered it was a queer place, so they walked and crept cautiously but were mystified. But Brett and younger brother really enjoyed the few minutes as they acted the landing of their space ship, helped by David H.

The movement period was often the indoor part of the lesson, but on some days the games-time was used for aspects that might help in the stimulation of work that may 'happen' in the writing period which followed.

The movement ideas were generally culled from several kinds of work that were in the minds of children. Brett was interested in rockets; Owen had been reading with Eric about mammoths and giant sloths; everyone had heard and talked about the poem read.

Each period offered the need for lessons for one group or another; and then letter-writing was taught in relation to the request for books from Miss Shortridge, who had written to most of the children about the books she sent them from the library a hundred miles away.

'Only one "t" in writen,' said Irene.

'I am writen a litter to you. How does that sound?' said someone.

'I don't have to say anything else after I have asked for my book, do I?' asked Mavis.

'Oh yes you do. Ask for one on pirates for me please?' asked Clifton.

'And another Madeline book would be good.'

Children went on with letters; and gradually, as the last of the morning moved nearer, most were engaged on their own writings of large stories which had become the most recent 'tradition' at the school. Some came to older children to talk about their story. One or two were painting or preparing lino cuts to illustrate them. Some of these stories were diaries of discoveries the children were engaged in at their home farms: David was writing up his experiments in taming eels, Mavis was doing a story on rats, and Dennis was telling about the old motorbike he and his brother were 'repairing'.

'I measured the cylinder and the ruler said two and a quarter inches, and I told the garage chap that's the size of the new cylinder he was to sell me. He told me I had to measure it in millimetres,' wrote Dennis.

Lunch interrupted the work, but Sarah looked as if she had had enough, for she was away to her lunch before the rest. Valerie, Ted, and Nell trailed out, along the half mile or so, home for lunch. Owen crouched beside Rosalie's bicycle, blowing up the tyre for her, not that he was a gallant, but rather to show off his ability. Soon she was along the road standing over her bicycle looking through the mail that the service car had left a few minutes before. Owen rushed past her on his way for his meal, late as usual. The other children from the far away Akatere Hills and Mangonui harbour farms sat in groups about the grounds in favourite places eating and talking.

The afternoon began with two plays. First there was the play of Ken's story about the ram that wouldn't be driven to the shearers. 'Martha, you be one of the shearers, and you too, if you like, Kathleen. And who would like to be the ram?'

'Me,' said most of them.

The play was produced and then discussed, as was usual.

'Too noisy in the wool-shed I think,' was Sarah's remark.

'Extra good,' was Eric's.

The other play was part of a large one which would run for over an hour. It was about the storming of a pa (fortified village) by members of early New Zealand militia, and about settlement in the North after that.

A talk was given by one of the boys, Owen, who was interested in the houses of the settlers of the valley of Oruaiti. He had been to see the one or two older people in the area and knew his own family's story well.

'Great grandfather came to the valley and lived away up the top where Miss F. lives. There was a house just next to the school, because I found the base of the chimney and one over the road too. Our other grandfather came from that one, but no one can tell me anything about the one by the football patch. I found some bits of old-fashioned bricks from the base. They are pierced with a dozen or so holes. They did that so the bricks would fire easier right into the middles. Here's one.' And Owen produced a soft worn and perforated brick.

'Excuse me, Owen, but I bet I could fire better bricks

in my kiln. I've rigged up an oil drip and I think I can get a good red heat in three hours,' said Tiger.

'But they didn't have oil. I suppose they used tea-tree.'

'Slabs from the mill probably would have been easier to get, and they wouldn't have cost anything.'

'Dad doesn't know a thing about the bricks,' said Rosalie. The coarse, crumbly, red, warped brick was looked at again.

'Why Mum has stacks of those. She uses them to go round her garden.'

'Our cream-shed has them in it too,' said Ted.

'I wonder if they were made by the early people at Mangonui or were they made out here?'

'Who could tell us?'

Eric was well into his nature records on a nest of centipedes he had found with his classmate, Clifton. 'You didn't see them, did you?' asked Eric. 'Little whity jokers with tiny almost useless legs, all together with their mother.'

'You didn't know their mother looked after them, did yer?'

'I'll show you. Come with me out to the glass house. They're under a heap of glass.'

'You're next with this book Necia.'

'Go on! It's a very good one.'

'But I got four already,' she said.

'This one won't keep. Anyway Mavis wants it too, so you better.'

So she did.

David went on with his plaster-mould positive, on to which he later poured plaster into a cardboard former. Mike set up his fabric on the printing table and began to finish off his day printing the final stencil on his crucifixion fabric. Many others drifted to the arts and crafts as the day reached its final period. Only one or two were talking when Bernard rang the bell, and then it was necessary to hold an assessment of the day's work.

Young David's painting, 'Wild Rabbits That Play', rested against the work-bench wall.

'I like the way he suggested the darkness in the burrows with drawn out lines in that particular colour.'

'It's good it follows the curves.'

'I think it needs more texture,' added Allan.

'It's a good painting, David, and I like it even if what Allan says is partly true,' said David W.

Martha's long story, with its interesting cover lay on the completion table with a few other short reports for the magazine people to look at next day.

'Here is the story we are going to hear tomorrow, isn't it?'

Eric's wooden mask lay on the table among a pile of reports and stories presented by the others. A new mask form by David and a few lino-prints and Lorna's long story also presented themselves for discussion.

'Eric waited till there were a lot of things on the table before he put his mask there,' said Dennis.

'Are you Eric or am I?' asked Eric quietly. 'I just happened to think it was right today, even if it did look finished to you yesterday. Anyway we've got such a lot of good things today that are finished, I thought it would make a good showing to put it in.' Aside to Ronny, 'Makes me feel good too.'

'Nothing wrong with that,' said Mary, 'although I haven't anything on the table today.'

> 'A long thin tune moved into the room
> And the feeling is with me still.'

And the feeling is with me still.

The day was over.

'What are you going to do now Owen? Would you come through our place on the way home and see my dam in the creek?'

'Good, Allan, but I have to get home to mow the lawns before five.'

They grabbed their bags and ran off together.

'Wait for me Allan,' said brother Colin.

'See you tomorrow, Rudolf.'

'Bring me a box tomorrow,' said someone. 'Wax ones are better.'

'I'm going to feed Jack, my eel, with rotten eggs now. Dennis, you take my bag and get the cows in for me.'

'You do as I tell you, or I'll tell Mum to sack you.'

In a few short minutes the valley children were away from the school gates in twos and threes on their way home.

'Hurry! The bus is going soon, Moana. Snowy, where are you?'

And soon the small bus had begun its journey through the back hill-country of Akatere, where it stopped at various muddy tracks that lead up to the homes of Sarah, Martha, Mary, Mike, and David.

At the open coast beach Irene, Mary, John, Sonny and the others trailed off with the little children behind them, along the flotsam line, the last mile home below the bush where the kiwi* cries, to their old stove that fumes flames and smoke through the cracks. And home, too, to all the thoughts and interests of a living that is just as much a part of their school.

* Wingless New Zealand bird

2

THE BEGINNING

WHEN I first came to this school the greater part of the valley foothills was covered with scrub, but almost all the river floodplain was farmed. Remnants of original bush remained in the deeper, wetter gullies high on the valley wall, where they were safe from the fires which still ranged from time to time.

I was curious about the plants that lived in these gullies, and one of my first thoughts was to cut tracks up to some of the clumps of trees, so that we could collect and cultivate plants that they contained. For a time we visited one bush patch and brought young trees back, but most of them died as our ground did not offer enough shelter from sun and weather. I did not think that there was any value in the ubiquitous species that made up the scrubland, and I directed the children only to the unusual plants. Later this led us to make occasional treks out of the valley to the original forest patches.

As we moved through the hilly scrub-country, again and again I stopped to examine the grey clays in the creek beds. I had a considerable interest in clay because

I looked forward to introducing pottery to the school, but as yet I had little technical knowledge of the processes involved. I drew the children's attention to the clays and discussed the qualities and beauties of these and the red ochreous earths that we found on the exposed ridges. As well I introduced the children to ideas of beauty in land form and native plants.

Our endeavours brought us together, but I did not then realise the educational value of the informality of our discussions on and after such trips.

The lessons we learnt in these first few months were real and valuable ones. We might have gone on and on making the same mistakes had I not a deep feeling about continuing some of the studies that did not work. The plant collecting and growing failed, and I saw that it was not only the unusual plant life that should engage us in our nature study. I saw that our interest in clay was real and valuable. I did not abandon the nature programme but modified it so that we studied the common species as well. We had found insects and other unusual organisms on these walks and were able to cover the needs of natural science in the school. I hoped that our clay investigation would lead us to a suitable clay for school pottery. This interest in botany and pottery in 1950 was my beginning.

Finally we found a seam of grey clay that we thought was much better than the others, and we took several loads back to school. It looked unpromising when we tipped it out on the small concrete square in front of the school. If we had not had the experience of collecting other inferior clays and mixing them to a workable consistency, we might have discarded this clay. Instead we chopped it up with a spade, watered it, and worked the mass with feet and hands into a clay of good quality. We had some clay to begin our pottery, but we thought we would make a survey of most clay deposits in the valley and then we would test the clays and see if one was better than another.

The children brought in a great number of samples. If they became over-enthusiastic about any one clay because it was more plastic than another only because it had been collected and maintained in a wetter condition, I drew their attention to the fact. I led them to see that we had to consider each sample in its working condition.

This led to methods of sampling. The children often found their enthusiasm running away with them when they visited the next deposit that they felt must be the best that could be found. As exaggerations crept in I taught more and more scientific method, so that we could ensure that the best clay was discovered. The important thing about all this study was that we were learning from each other about the material and our valley. We were also learning about the clay by experiments that involved growing judgement. The teaching was reflected in later studies of temperature in the air, in the shade, and in the river. When we began a study of the river the children devised methods of sampling the water which were quite scientific.

Rex, a senior boy at that time, wheeled his mother's barrow the mile up the valley to the school. I had arranged that at last we would stockpile our raw material and begin pottery. We were waiting with spades and sacks to begin the work. His barrow contained some of the first of many bricks that the children brought to the school in order to make the kiln. Soon we set out.

'No work,' said Nancy, 'and all morning too.'

'No-o-o-o work,' said Trevor who enjoyed the idea of dispensing with formal lessons.

I remember watching the children moving along the grass fringe of the road in an informal happy way and wondering at their enthusiasm and their definition of work. I knew very well that this was work, but of a different sort. The children were keen, perhaps too keen, for David pushed into Trevor and over they both went. There were roars of laughter. Great fun this! No work today!

A strong spirit of the outdoors engaged us as we came to the clay bank, but there was a stronger purposefulness than in the classroom, created by their enthusiasm and the discipline of the investigation. I appreciated and enjoyed their conversation, perhaps for the first time fully.

'This is about the same as Mary's sample from her place.'

'But this won't quite twist around my finger . . . Look! . . . It cracks.'

'Wet it more. My one is all right.'

'That's not a thrush; it's a brown blackbird, a hen.'

'Could we make a test tile out of this band?'

'Don's pigs stink.'

' "Brown blackbirds," Really! Attar of pigs! What next?'

'I'll push the first load,' said Joy.

As well as the loads that were carried back to the brick bin at the school we took back with us several pound samples of clay that we wished to use for testing, so that we could 'prove' our deposit. Slowly the bin was filled, 'toed down', and watered, and then covered.

The first day at pottery arrived. Varley clawed at the roughly mixed clay in the bin, sprinkled shards on a board, squeezed a handful of clay in his hands, regathered the extruded bits and contemplated what he had in hand to mix. He reconsidered the effort and threw a large piece back into the bin. Others were mixing quietly, building up a reserve of mixed clay so that they could make a large part of their pot before having to mix again. Bevin was thinking he would make a large heap of snakes as Kelvin did one day when we used the 'old' clay.

Pots, Trevor, 12 years

'Dad's getting the new tractor I told you about,' said Alma.

'Not as good as ours,' said Lois, and with chatter of this sort coil was joined to coil and pots and figures grew. Trevor, who had been working at speed was thrilled, for he had his pot eighteen inches high and it was still growing, but soon he had to hold the sides so that it did not sag. The coils became looser as he manipulated them, and his eagerness increased till, with a

17

shout from Neville and Pearl, the whole pot slumped to the table. For Trevor the pot was a tremendous success. He was overjoyed. Then he began again, with caution, and a pot rose that was firm and solid but not as high as the one that had thrilled him and the others a short time before.

Later, Trevor planned a group of shapes he was going to make during the week, and he assessed the amount of clay he would need. He then collected his clay and prepared it so that he would have an unbroken time at constructing the pots he planned. This was the way the keener potters worked.

I saw that there was much boisterousness from one section of the class at that time. However I felt that this good fun was valuable experience. Often there is a similar outcry of noise in the beginning of creative work. This process appeared valuable from another point of view also, in that there was really an active discussion of values going on. The potters talked about form and decoration as they worked. They were also establishing each other's individuality as persons with this power to know and express opinion. There was a new form of discipline and responsibility to the people and materials which I had not seen before. The work itself appeared to maintain a new control over the individuals.

The clay we used was not good, and in the first months a large number of pots cracked in drying. We returned to scientific method to solve the problem. We tried several ways of storing and drying them. We dried some rapidly in the stove, and these all cracked badly. The ones that were sun-dried also cracked, but those which were placed in the dark of the store room cupboard and dried slowly did not crack at all. We found that bottoms cracked unless we turned the pots early in the process of drying. We enjoyed these experiments, and found that this sort of work added considerable purpose to our discussion. I began to feel that the result of this sort of study of real problems was true education.

Another problem that arose was how to deal with the large unmixed lumps that the clay commonly contained. I found it better to have them removed. Experience showed me, too, that it was best to provide a target for them on the fence rather than allow the children to select their own. We had already begun regular discussions on behaviour and rules, in order to work out a system of values that suited us. We found it interesting that the same group of children saw that it was they who were involved in most breaches of discipline. These were the few who wanted to throw clay, and since we worked in an open-air shelter-shed this relaxation seemed in order. I found that I could solve a great number of behaviour problems such as these by allowing the children the opportunity to discuss and solve the situation by some sort of resolution of energies.

I noticed that it did not seem necessary for a child to end a period with a pot or figure every time. Trevor gained considerable satisfaction from his pot-building to the point of collapse, and he enjoyed even this when the inevitable took place. The children recognised this as a sort of experimentation, and some of the best pots were made by those who were habitual experimenters. However as the practice of planning a pot became generally accepted, much of this experimentation ceased. On the other hand it is very important that a child who has a pot unfinished at the end of the day should be allowed time to complete it on the following day. This principle applies to any valuable task.

The children sketched pots that were most ingenious, but in many cases the pots did not arrive at the shape sketched. It appeared that the planning served only for a general sorting-out of ideas. However, a child would often say he wanted to make a particular shape and would do so at once. At other times I have seen children start off to make a particular shape but modify it again and again as they worked.

We collected some of the red earths from the ridges and mixed them up with water into slips. This was used to decorate the pots, and the children also drew designs into the clay on to the raw surface as well as through the red slip to cream coloured surface below. Sometimes they pressed a stick form into the surface.

I have always been amazed at the child's intuitive ability to get the feeling of a particular form or surface

Decorated pot, Joyce, 10 years

by a few experimental strokes of the brush in the air above the pot.

It seems that if he hasn't any particular idea in mind the area 'dictates' its own needs. The artist then, without hesitation, is able to apply the first stroke of the design. He reconsiders this and is able to add further strokes which 'demand' other wide or narrow lines or forms. The child seems to know intuitively what the needs of a given form are, and he knows when the design is complete. I have noticed how certain children, usually those who have been denied such satisfaction as these, will at first over-decorate a pot to the point of spoiling it, but if they are allowed repeated satisfaction from the craft they soon work with skill and taste.

The young potters were interested in the technique of scratching through coloured slip into base clay. They usually accented the basic line of the design. I noticed that they made use of unintentional discoveries of technique during decoration. Thus they explored sgraffito technique through common clay and various slip decorations; but none of these techniques were taught. The children discovered them as the need arose. New children who came later absorbed this information and soon were just as skilled.

The first pots that the children made were usually decorated with leaves, trees, seed shapes, fish, seaweeds, and more rarely flowers. As they became more confident in their approach to design they began to use related line, mass, colour, and texture in an abstract way.

Pot by Kelvin

I saw a good deal of cliché decoration on the first pots. I was careful however, to make my comments about the good aspects of the work, for I believed that by so doing I would encourage the work along the right lines in the quickest manner.

From the beginning very definite attitudes to clay work were noticeable. A dozen or so children who were enthusiasts spent all their spare time at some part of this activity, such as turning the drying pots or preparing a new batch of clay. These people were potters. They were also young authorities on the subject and could discuss the work done with increasing skill and awareness of the values of the pottery. I do not mean that they learnt values of appreciation; rather do I suggest that they developed inherent abilities that they had neglected to use until we became engaged on such a programme.

There were also a few, and not all the same people, who found a creative outlet in building, stacking, and the process of firing the kilns. They considered it their privilege to attend to every firing and to watch and stoke often late into the night. There were times when I had to take the tired stokers home and return to complete the firing. No child was unaffected by some activity in the chain, and there was no one who did not at some time make pots that were considered by the other children to be of the finest order.

The boys were the really keen potters, kiln builders, and firers; but two girls, Joyce and Pearl, were outstanding.

These children were particularly interested in the clay activity as a whole, and their natural understanding of the media helped them to overcome any technical difficulties as they arose. It was through this group of confident potters, both boys and the girls, that the advance into large pot construction and the development of controlled and fitting decoration were made.

The established pattern of work with clay continued for some time, till one day two boys came to me and suggested that they make some really huge pots.

'Instead of making four or five, as I like to sometimes, I think it would be really far more fun to make one huge one,' said Trevor.

'We'll have to roll coils quite differently,' added Bevin, who was already considering the new technical approaches needed for handling large pots. This was a new point of departure and was most important and interesting for all the children. It was a natural enough extension, but it is one that is often disregarded because of expense of materials or the technical problems involved.

Each of the boys prepared a large bin of clay, mixed it with more coarse brick-powder than usual and as well added liberal amounts of the woolly seed-heads of the native bullrush, raupo. This was added to strengthen the clay so that the pot would hold its shape as greater heights were reached. The pounding of the fired shards or brick and the collection of the raupo heads from the swamps became an added part of the activity. The

Pot by Bevin

Kelvin coiling a large pot

prepared coils were large, and the handling and thumping down of each coil involved new hand techniques. When the coils began to rise on the form it was found most convenient to sling long coils over the shoulder so that both hands were free for the thumping down of the mass after flattening. This process gradually assumed a rhythmic pattern as the potters shuffled around their growing pots.

Control of the form and the techniques of coiling were far easier for the children than with the small pots, and it was obvious that the entire process was a far more pleasurable one. The preparation of a large bin of clay did present problems until we discovered that we could work large heaps of clay with the feet. The 'grog' and raupo could be added during the re-heaping process.

Bevin, Trevor, Leslie and Kelvin went to the bins with clay boards and began portering clay back to the mixing table.

'Bevin, you and I'll have this bin,' said Kelvin.

'Oh, go on!' said Leslie, 'It's mine.'

There was no time nor wish to start a quarrel. The three began to roll long 'snakes' two inches thick and often a yard or so long. These they coiled like long cobras into their bins and in an hour they began rolling out large slabs of clay for pot bases on boards covered with brick dust.

'Watch me, Les,' said Bevin as he took a yard-long roll, slung it over his shoulder, hunched himself to take the weight evenly, and rhythmically stamped and

Pot by Kelvin

23

thumped the coil down into place as he moved around the slab.

'Like ramming a post, eh Les?'

'If you leave that crack between the coils, Bevin, your post will fall to bits.' A pause . . .

'How's that for thumbing?' said Kelvin as he clawed a large swipe of clay off a side to trim it to shape.

The sides slowly grew until the pots were fourteen or fifteen inches high and the potters had difficulty in looking into their shapes.

Then they climbed on boxes and continued coiling. Regularly they punched out the sides, sometimes plastered more clay on a thin place and leaned back to look and talk.

'How's it look from your side?'

'Bong it out there a bit,' said Trevor, who had finished his lunch and was beginning to mix a further batch of clay.

'Pearl wants to make one too,' said Trevor.

'A lot of work, Trev!' said Les.

Meanwhile Kelvin was leaning over his pot peering into the dark inside.

'Aaaaaah—a crack . . . Oh, ohoh, oooooh! Hey did you hear that?' he said as he began to speak into the hollowness of his pot.

'Trevor, listen . . . Ooooh, wooooo, wooooo!'

Kelvin continued booing and oohing into the depths of his pot while Leslie held his ear to the mouth of his and slapped the wet clay sides lightly and rhythmically.

Varley, Linda and Colin press moulding and clay mixing

The noise fun went on, until most of them climbed down and ate their lunches. They sat around their pots and talked about the new experiences, particularly the sounds they could make with the pots. They spoke of the satisfactions there were in clawing handfuls of clay off a pot to trim it to form, and that of 'bonging' a wall out to correct contour.

Slowly the pots were closed in nearly to completion. I was interested to see the way they scraped their pots into the desired shape at this stage, and I encouraged their vigorous use of sticks, boards, or finger tips.

Kelvin prepared some experimental lips for his pot, set one into place and stood off from his box, rejected it in a flash but built up a second into a perfected and completed form.

Meanwhile the others grew, eight large pots in all, each of some twenty to thirty pounds weight. The shapes were smoothed off, but not with water. The children saw that pots of these dimensions required a textured surface that did not look overworked. The decoration required much more decisive strokes. Most pots relied on the basic strength of a few strokes, and over-elaboration was rarely found.

There was always a large audience during such a session to watch the transformation of clay into pots. There were murmurs of approval. Sometimes someone doubted a particular development and a discussion ensued. Generally there was someone in the audience who wanted to make a pot.

Ever since then, there has always been someone who asks to make a very large pot. This has kept fresh these particular satisfactions. During the years following, other clay techniques have been developed, but no better work has been done than when the children made the first kiln of giant pots.

I found it necessary to introduce the technique of plaster moulds. The process of pressing clay into a plaster form, smoothing-off, designing, and decorating was easily grasped by the children. A feature of this method was that the mould-pressing process allowed the child to press the clay in a very relaxed way. Rhythmic pressing processes much like kneading were developed. Later I used this process as an introductory clay activity for a group of entrants because I knew that it would allow them to make high quality pottery quickly without having first to learn the coiling process.

The children soon developed satisfactory thumbing, palm pressing, and finger working methods for themselves. They discussed the way their hands could be used and I joined with them in their enjoyment of these discoveries of the satisfaction of movement. This lead them on to textural experimentation on clay. I had just introduced the children to oil paints and there was a good deal of carry-over of principle and technique. I did not teach techniques here, but when a child found a new way of using his hands, brushes, and clay, I assisted him to realise his discovery and this led to others seeing and trying too. For example, if a child found out that a sawn end of timber could make waving scraped lines in clay and give a good textural surface, I encouraged the child to use this knowledge when he painted as well as in his pottery. We were able to prepare hundreds of textured tiles which recorded the many discoveries we had made. Many natural surfaces such as bark, leaves, timber, and shells were also used to press into clay surfaces. A few children pressed in small branched twigs, but most made up their own textural surface by some sort of scraping, drawing, pressing, or brushing. Some of the potters working at moulds, in particular Varley, derived added satisfaction from working clay into moulds without watching or with closed eyes.

A few children have always preferred press-mould work, and although I hesitate to say that these were the ones who had a greater interest in design and decoration, in many cases it did seem so. There have also been two or three rather insecure children who liked the controlled work of mould-making and clay-pressing.

There came a time when the drying pots filled the shelves to overflowing.

The pots were turned regularly and finally were bone dry. The children returned to look over their pots and re-lived the satisfactions they had enjoyed as they made them. As well they came to look at other people's work. Varley came up to the shelves one day and turned a pot nimbly in his fingers. He peered rather short-sightedly as was his habit, then he put it down.

'No, it's too heavy, and the lip's not quite drawn in enough, but that's a lovely brush stroke here.'

He moved on to another pot of his own. I could see he liked that pot a lot. Many children came in to look over their pots and to make judgements that involved real values. I noted a growing respect and care with the work of others, and it was interesting that the children asked that very special pots and figures should be put away in a cupboard where they would be preserved and would not run the risk of being damaged.

We had enough bricks collected by this time to begin building a kiln. We made a small bottle-kiln shortly after. It was very simple and rather crudely built: steel supports held up the fire-port brick arches, and we had to unload the kiln from the top, which meant a certain amount of dismantling. There were three small fire-ports around the base of the bee-hive, and we had worked out an arrangement to fire the kiln from the chimney as well.

We stacked all the pots we had made into the base of the kiln supported on a few bricks, and sealed up the chimney stack with ashes, sand, and clay mixture. We had gathered a large heap of wattle and pine logs and branches beside the kiln and were then ready to fire the next day.

The valued articles all were inside the kiln. The shelves were bare except for a few 'green' pots. The hopes of every child and the success of the whole idea rested on the next day's work, and the three small fires that would be lit at dawn the next day. I had little idea how to fire a kiln but I knew that the firing had to be slow at first until the water had been driven off the pots. I felt sure that we would have considerable losses and had prepared the children for this.

Rex and Neville sat around the small ports and fed sticks into the fires ever so slowly, so that the fires rarely swept up into the chamber. By the time we arrived for school they had the kiln warm but little more, except where the fires burned in the ports. They raked the fires when they appeared to be too large and fed them as they died down. Hour after hour they worked, slowly bringing the flames up and up until the time came to load large branches and limbs end on, into the ports. Flames were roaring up through the pottery by then and the wedges of clay used to block the chimney cracks were shrinking away from the bricks.

'Was that a bang, Neville?' asked Rex anxiously, 'or was it a stick blowing up?'

'Rake the fires quick, rake 'em quickly, it's pots blowing up,' yelled Neville. Well, they raked and built up the fires until they became less and less anxious about the various bangs that continued to come from the fires and or the pottery within. They more or less gave up and went on firing pretending that the bangs were really only sticks. They spoke of 'clay bangs' and 'wood bangs' and seemed to know which was which but I felt somewhat confused by these sounds and was worried in that I didn't seem to see the differences as they did.

By lunch time there were flames gushing out of the hundreds of cracks all over the kiln. We then began to throw small branches and sticks down the chimney and gradually the flames built up to a roar. Pine cones and larger branches were added, and as the afternoon wore on we saw bricks glowing dull red. This was exciting for we knew that our pottery, whatever was left of it would now be nearly fired.

We stoked, repaired, threw more branches in, levered larger logs into the firing ports, and dull thuds continued to come from within. Everyone helped, even the little ones like Eric and Mary until late in the afternoon all had grown very weary; and most of us were so despondent at the list of thuds and 'clay bangs' that had been recorded as scratches on a brick that we were ready to give up. We closed over the ports with sods of earth, lifted the end of a benzine drum over the chimney, and we left it. None of us knew what we had done. We knew what we wanted to do and had an idea that we would get something approximating brick in appearance when the morning came, but that was all.

When I saw the kiln the next morning I was miserable. It looked so crude and dirty, blackened with smoke, with swirls of ash in the air around the ports. I prepared the children for the worst, for I felt that these few bricks must contain ruined fragments of the pottery they valued so much.

'Look at the clay that we parged the kiln with. It's turned to earthenware. Yes, keep some bits. It's

27

wonderful what has happened to it. It's no longer clay. We couldn't turn it back to clay even if we wanted to,' I added.

'It's earthenware,' said Joe.

Rex lifted off the benzine drum-end, and we began to lift off the cooler upper bricks and toppled the hotter lower ones to the ground.

'Look out, Joe! They're still hot . . . Not yet, Mavis! They don't cool that quickly . . . They would make good hot-water bottles, wouldn't they?' Slowly we prized them off, pushed them out of the way with sticks, and lower and lower the structure went until Rex ventured to look over the chimney into the ash mass below.

'They're still there! Yes, they're there! One's whole. It's yours, Trev. Oh, it's hot!' He reeled back as a swirl of ash and smoke blew into his face.

'I'd like a look.'

'Me too!'

'After you, Eva!'

The baked earthenware daubing clinkered about our feet, as caution was cast aside. Hands wrapped in handkerchiefs threw bricks away, and soon we saw the heap of pottery covered with ash, with here and there a pot showing through. They were burnt to a good light biscuit with the red slip decorations a dark rich red and not one piece was 'dunted', chipped, or 'clay banged'. We dug in the hot ashes, and for an hour or so we looked over every piece and discussed the exciting results.

The empty shelves were refilled with fired pottery, and they have been refilled and emptied many, many times since. The pots have been better, the firings have been just as perfect, but this discovery of the firing process made the beginning of pottery a wonderful experience. Every heart was full.

The process of pottery-making itself is very important. I feel sure that the quality of the work as well as the technical advancements made by the group were related to the activity as a whole.

I spoke to the children about comparable discoveries in primitive societies, and for some time we learnt about the discovery of fire, iron, bronze, and steel, and we melted various low-melting metals in simple 'forges', bringing an understanding to these studies that we had not known before.

The children began other crafts known to ancient and primitive peoples. Varley and Trevor made wood and wire sculpture heads as well as lino blocks and paintings. Neville made a Polynesian canoe complete with block-printed 'tapa' cloth sails.

The pottery and figures stayed on shelves for some time, and regularly the children came back to admire the work and to handle it. They were critical of the pots, and their discussions of the values of the work seemed very sensible to me. Sometimes a child did not give a very comprehensive evaluation of a pot, but I saw that they knew. As well, they appeared to retain this ability to make assessments of the value of a thing

Native head design by Varley

long after leaving the primary school and ceasing to do creative work. Four years after, Varley came back to see what the later pupils had been doing. In the same way as when he was a boy, he indicated the good and sorted through the work to find strengths. He did this with confidence and skill.

'The top is too fat there, and I think the colour could be darker,' he would say. Varley undoubtedly derived more satisfaction than most from the work we did, for he continued to maintain an active contact with the school for as long as I stayed in the valley.

He helped at every firing of the various kilns, and at times he wrote short poems or observations on his experiences.

'I wrote this the other day,' he would say; or 'I cut this out from a bit of box wood. I thought you might like to show the children.'

'I would like to mount it on very black fine-grained wood, but I haven't got any.'

I was very interested in one aspect of his continued expression. His style of language was much the same as he had used years ago when he was at school. The important thing, however, was that he continued to know the value of things, and I think that this ability resulted in large degree from the pottery activity and the feeling for material gained over a number of years.

We rebuilt the kiln about a year later and made 'saggars' in which to place ware for glazing with low-temperature lead glazes. The kiln was too unreliable. Often 'good pots' did not 'come out', or the glaze melted and 'treacled' down the sides in an unsightly way. Generally the children felt that the glazes were not desirable, but they found that it made their pottery more acceptable at home. 'Some pots need glaze, and most don't,' was Mary's comment. We couldn't understand the glaze firing process, and except for rare occasions we gave up glazing. Later, however, we built a small stoneware kiln which we used to fire high-temperature glazes. The glaze materials were collected locally. Silica sands and various ashes were made from selected grasses and woods. We used crude oil to get the higher temperature, and the results were certainly better than the lead glazes of the past.

Five years later we arrived at a new beginning, when fifteen children came from a far-away school. These people disliked school and lacked ability and the desire to express themselves. They came into an atmosphere in which creative work was developed to include art, crafts, creative writing, poetry, drama, dance, and some number activity. Their attainments were below standard, and they felt that they could never do good work. I introduced them to pottery, and a programme was worked out for the remaining two terms of the year. Their coiled pottery was very limited, but generally they extended their work in size and quality, but it was the plaster-mould work that really brought out their confidence. Plaster pressings may not be a very expansive medium for ceramic work, but the amount of confidence that the process gave these pupils was great. They enjoyed filling large areas with designs, and all gained satisfaction from their efforts. One of the really good things about press moulds was the especial suitability of the large open areas for decoration.

The satisfactions enjoyed here were sufficient to encourage them to improve their ability and interest in coiled pottery. The new children had not the slow build-up over many years of pottery activity, and they had missed the discussions and experimentation that we had been involved in over these years. The mould processes

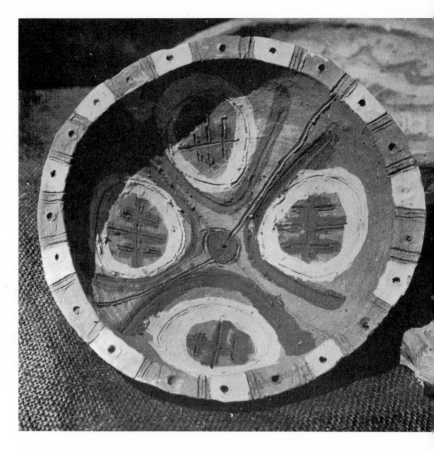

Press moulded bowl by Bernard

31

gave them satisfactions which assisted them to overcome these omissions and do coiled work comparable to the work of others.

I felt that one boy, Nick, who came later, was probably a person who had never known the satisfaction of having made a thing for himself. He had begun many tasks but had never finished them, and as I watched him attempting to work in clay I saw that he must be helped to end up with a pot that day.

I encouraged him, and then in near desperation I asked Nell to help Nick finish his pot. Together they completed a simple cylinder. The children were genuinely thrilled to see the crude, but finished pot and praised him.

'Good on you, Nick! I like straight-sided cylinder pots.'

'Cylinders are my favourite form,' said Helen.

'Design it, Nick,' said David.

David showed him how to scratch through the red slip and told him about the various coloured slips. First, he painted over the whole pot with red slip and applied layer after layer of slip (and energy) to it. Slowly it grew like a piece of mould. He scratched through the slip, designing it at various levels of painting, but I could see that he was thrilled as ever he could be with it. The pot was subjected to about every indignity it could take, until at the end of the day he had finished. Nick was expansively happy at his creative work, and he had been acclaimed by the group. This assisted him in his general behaviour in the school, and as long as he received satisfaction of this order he behaved well, whereas previously he had behaved badly.

Over the years it became necessary to return to starting points and build afresh. These new beginnings are vitally important to the process of continuous growth. Each re-beginning in pottery has been different, but each time, even though I know too well the processes involved, I have attempted to preserve some of the feeling of discovery that we knew at the first firing. I continued to value the activity and knew this to be largely the reason for the pottery successes.

Other beginnings have been with a stone-ware kiln and later a large salt-glaze kiln designed by a craft potter. At the height of the last pottery resurgence Barry Brickell, a craft potter, visited us. The children and he sat amongst the pots and talked about pottery.

'Now this *is* a pot, honest and full of life. What a lovely fireburn on this side, and the design certainly fits the shape and the form, doesn't it? You made it, Kelvin? Beautiful work!'

'Now this person is a real potter. I can see that at once. He knows the feel of clay and has done as much with this piece of clay as I think he could have.'

It was a wonderful experience for the young people, and the sort of one they should have, and Barry told me afterwards it was a wonderful one for him too.

3

MORE BEGINNINGS

BY the time that pottery had been established I had observed enough of the children's manner of work to know that I could learn much from them and that any preconceived ideas I had of the way in which their expression would develop were likely to lead me astray. After the pottery experiences and the success we knew with the first firing of the kiln I felt sure that their experience could be extended to other crafts and arts, and that if I introduced new media they surely would have much to 'say' with the material.

I wanted the children to have experiences in line, form, colour, texture, and space. I did not think that everyone should necessarily work in materials that engaged all these aspects of art and craft at once, but I felt rather that certain children would favour particular aspects. This led me to introduce lino-cutting, fabric printing, oil, tempera painting, crayon, paint and dye painting, relief and impression tile and plaque making, mobiles and sculpture work. In the beginning I knew less than the children about these materials. I was dependent for my knowledge of some of these processes

on the instruction of W. R. Allen and E. C. Seelye. I was fortunate in that both of these also believed firmly in the creative power of children. Often I have gone back to a comment of Seelye's: 'Let's go back and see what the children have to say about it.' It is surprising how often this has solved a problem.

First I introduced lino cutting. I was not troubled that this medium offered experience in incision in line, nor concerned that it offered opportunities in line, form, texture and colour. I felt that the new set of problems this medium presented was the important thing.

We tried out the new cutters and showed each other what we found out, but I did not set any subject for the children. I was surprised by the flood of cliché boats, yachts, liners, coral islands, aeroplanes spitting bullets (no pilots), speedboats also spitting bullets again without drivers, and the occasional cowboy drawing a six-shooter. I watched this rash of unrelated expression with considerable anxiety. These were the children who had been making such sensitive and delightful pots. I allowed this cliché statement to go on for a time. I suppose there was almost everything wrong with the first

four or five cuts apiece: areas were unfilled and vacant, others were cut away completely and appeared 'lost', cliché rendering of figures as stick-men were common, and all in all the results left me downhearted. However, the children slowly tired and began to take more interest in filling in a block.

At this stage I began to praise the good things that appeared in their work. Mary put a little bird at the bottom of her fast, driverless-car block, and I praised her for it and drew the children's attention to similar good things in each lino cut. Soon I found that others were recognising good things and were pointing out things to me that I had not noticed. Then a few began to select subjects from the environment for their work. In this way the first prints of horses, thrushes, tractors, and trees appeared on our walls. We put them there because we saw that we had to have a place for the better things to be on display, because we knew already of the stimulative influence this had in making us do further work.

At this point we began regular nature walks to the river, to the bush, and to the beach. These rambles led to many discoveries. Nell's *Water Snail Eggs on a Stone* was one of the first lino blocks that resulted from such a nature walk. Nature study took on a new importance. I concentrated my attention on introducing new topics to the children, and we became more and more discriminating in our walks and activities generally. Thus we re-visited a bird we had observed in a particular tree and

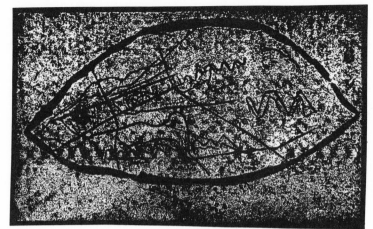

Water snail eggs on a stone by Nell

1518075

went back at regular times to look at the development of the snail eggs. We returned regularly to see a large fern-shoot as it slowly uncurled and developed into a mature frond. Much lino work resulted from such activities, and very slowly the children began to select more and more of their own topics of interest. I saw the familiar stimulative process starting off: one child did a willow tree lino block that was good, and this stimulated another to do one, and so on until many had attempted the subject. At all times there was a close relationship between the study we were doing in the field and the lino cutting in the school.

Soon nearly all the lino work was based on nature

subjects, and cliché subjects appeared less and less: Lois aged 9 did *Willows*, and Trevor aged 11 cut his *Cabbage Tree*. Trevor's cut followed a certain amount of research on the trees, and it indicates that he had found out that the dead leaves hang on the trees for years and that the flowers hang down and are partly protected when young by the overhanging green leaves. He saw that the ground was hummocky and that a tree usually grew on a mound. The other mounds proved to have had trees on them too.

Cabbage tree, Trevor

Willow, Lois

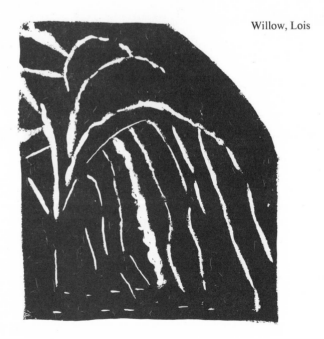

Trevor saw that the land could have been swampy and had sunk away from the tree mounds in the past.

The topic, *Tree*, as illustrated by David I.'s *Manuka Tree*, Bevin's *Willows*, and Owen's *Tree* and *Wattle*, is part of a gradual growth of interest in all kinds of trees. I was interested in the diverse styles of their cuts: no

36

Tree, Owen, 9 years   Manuka tree, David W., 7 years   Wattle, Owen, 9 years

two were alike. Lois's poetic *Willow* was very different from the rather 'scientific' cut of Trevor's and this from the strong feeling of David's *Manuka*. The link with the nature rambles and the scientific observation that I instigated in the classroom was very strong, and when such individual studies were started I usually followed with a small lesson, for instance about one of the trees or the snails.

Subject after subject was exploited in our work and lino blocks were done of dogs, roosters, birds, trees, animals, fish, the river, and as other school subjects exerted their influence there were interpretations of

Pine tree by Allan

Willow by Bevin

poems, stories, and social studies subjects. In the main subjects were taken from the environment. David I.'s *Dog Design*, Nell's *Water Snail Eggs on a Stone*, and Valerie's (age 7) *Crying*, arose out of this. For a time lino work displaced the intense interest in pottery, though this continued. I found that particular children went on with pot making, and others seemed to prefer lino work.

Many of the early statements were incomplete and were begun and finished with the same-sized cutter. It was amazing how long a child would continue to work with the same tool every time he chose to do a lino block. Again I drew the children's attention to the blocks such as David's *Manuka Tree*, where he has used several different cutters and has filled in the areas well. We spoke of 'balanced' pictures, and these discussions after a day's work, that had become so much a part of our approach, generally drew attention to the satisfactions of well filled blocks and pictures. I had observed the way children know where to place a line or a shape when they decorate a pot, and now I could see that they had the same feeling of 'rightness' when they approached the discussion of a lino block or a painting.

Some of the younger children persisted in using the one cutter and I saw that this was not necessarily a bad thing. Allan's *Pine Tree*, is probably all the more interesting because he has done this. This happened with other blocks too: Lois's *Willows*, David's *Dog Design*, and Valerie's *Crying*. I was then careful to see that the children realised that it may not always be necessary for them to use many cutters. I knew how easy it was for me to over-direct and hold up their development by applying technical knowledge before they needed it. I remembered the textural knowledge the children had found out in their pottery work, and I wondered whether they would develop the blocks into larger sizes at some stage, as they had done in their pottery. I knew that two- and three-colour blocks would be possible and that tinting with dyes of the white areas could give effect to block prints. However, this came later, and at that time it did not seem that there was any likelihood of such development.

It was about this time that I asked the children to write about their work as well, so that they could share their thoughts and discoveries with others. Sharing was

Crying, Val, 7 years

Dog design by David W.

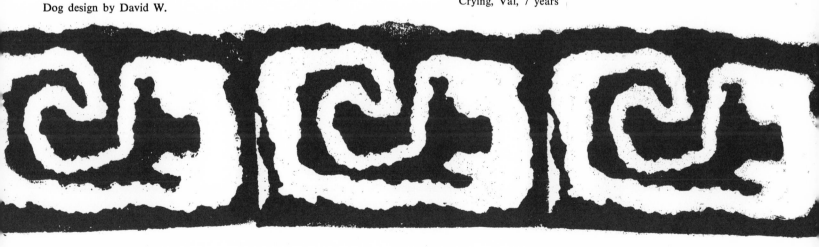

necessary at this time, for more and more children were engaged on studies of their own or in small groups. There was the need for reports on different projects.

Some of this need was satisfied by the talks about the art and lino work. Trevor studied the cabbage tree, Allan joined him, and this led to others, until most of the children had been with him on one of his investigations.

I did not give instructions before the children began writing, nor did I choose subjects for them. If they chose to write about a bird they were studying, I encouraged them to think about the possibilities of doing a lino block or a painting with it. Sometimes the story was written after the picture. I revised the poetry that I introduced to children then, and was careful to exclude all poetry especially written by adults for children. To some extent I followed this pattern in the short stories that I read to the classes, but saw that the stories of such writers as Kipling and Kenneth Grahame and others like them were valuable. In nearly all cases we felt that this adult writing especially written for children was a poor substitute for their own expression and that the influence of that sort of work was likely to hold up natural development of children. As well, it was more than likely that 'childish' poetry and story would destroy children's ability to know good work from bad.

The children were not asked to write in any particular style, whether of poetry or prose. I thought that the feeling of the picture, or the lino block, or the circumstances of their observation would be enough to assist the child to make his choice, and I was prepared to allow him to say what his writing was, whether poetry or prose.

The first poetry received was in the same vein as the poetry that the children knew from lessons.

THE THRUSHES
The thrush sings all day
But doesn't have any pay.
He flies in the bush.
His colour is bright
But you cannot see him at night
They aren't very nice to us.
LESLIE

Leslie couldn't have been more inaccurate in his statement about thrushes. His poem contained most of the erroneous and senseless statements that come of the need to make the rime. His lino cut was printed at three stages of cutting, until at last he arrived at the satisfactory print.

'What do you think of the bird here, Alma? Any good?' he asked.

'Hmmm, room for the sun! What about some branches to fill up that gap?'

I saw that the lino work, pottery, and painting would improve rapidly because of this kind of discussion, but that the language work would not develop in the same way because of the difficulty of putting the same process into effect.

I found it difficult to see anything approaching 'the little bird at the foot of a lino block' that I could praise the children for in the pages and pages of writings done in those first weeks. The 'driverless boats' and 'aeroplanes-in-flames' stage of lino cliché experience were bad enough, but this new thing in language seemed worse. Then Neville, who was working on gum trees for his tree study wrote a new sort of poem that still contained a trace of rime.

This poem was so much better than the others, not only because it rested for its success on a more subtle internal rime, but also because it made sense and was a statement of *truth* about the tree.

THE GUM TREES

The gum trees have berries brown
Which in the autumn
Fall to the ground
And spread around like powder
By the hour.

NEVILLE

Neville's poem was much better than the rimed poems that the children persisted in producing. Their prose writings contained a good number of accepted phrases and statements from everyday usage. I made a quick assessment of the work done so far and concluded that I need not be unduly concerned that the standard of their writings appeared much worse than the work they had been doing in formal English (See Chapter 5, Language Development). I saw that the quality of work had changed and felt that the children were throwing out clichés and would be likely to develop their own idiom soon. I saw that the apparent deterioration of standards could not be blamed on this approach, for we had been working for very few weeks, nor did I see how it could

The thrush by Leslie

be through a lapse in the ability to be expressive. I didn't think that the work indicated the children's real ability as yet. Neville's poem was the first piece that indicated sincerity. Perhaps Neville's poem was nearer the real value of children's writing. The previous work was probably insincere, and the new was more likely to be sincere. I felt then that I understood Leslie and the others.

In the creative approach to learning I have found numerous stages such as this, where the way ahead does not seem clear. The unplanned approach seems so contrary to one's desire to move ahead. Planning however could quite easily hinder development.

The influence of adult poetry with regular rime and rhythm patterns continued to influence the children's work. I did not understand the problem of these skills as yet and was not prepared to say that children had indicated that they did not necessarily want to use rime in their poetry. Some children slowly began to abandon rime, but others persisted.

THE GORSE AND ME
Oh the gorse as it stings
When it pricks into many things.
When I disturb them
How they determine the soft places,
Leaving all the traces.
NEVILLE

At this time the success of any poem was often measured in the use of natural and unforced rime, and I saw that if this was the manner of children's poetry it was clear that there would be few children who would become poets. I saw that nearly all the poetry that I was reading to the classes was adult rimed verse and that our attention was being directed towards expecting sincere and unforced use of rime in our writings. I saw too that most children were writing poetry and not prose in our writing periods. This was probably because the children were expressing feeling, and I thought that this would be likely to direct them to poetry rather than prose. Although the frequency of clear and acceptable thought in poems soon began to increase, a great deal of the 'not so good' was the result of this error in approach.

As often as not, the particular thought a child had in mind should have been written in prose. We decided in one of our discussion periods that we would restrict our discussions to the work selected by the child to be read aloud, and we would not force ourselves to write poetry to the exclusion of stories. Then they began to write in forms that suited their needs.

I recognised rhythm patterns appearing in poetry for some time after I gave up compelling children to learn certain poetry off by heart. I considered that this expression of rhythms was possible due to too great an emphasis on a particular poem. A great deal of this influence had to be worked out by the writers before they could express themselves with clarity and individuality.

Fish in weeds, Michael, 13 years

WAY OUT

Way out at sea
So far outside.
No sign of bee to see
So far out at sea.

Where the waves crash on large rocks
There our small boat do'st glide
So far out at sea.

The rocks do'st hide beneath the sea,
Where our boat will crash
So far out at sea.

VARLEY

We began to collect sayings that we thought were valuable and interesting: Mavis saw a reflection in a puddle and said, 'I see the upside down world.' Joyce, talking about her dog, said, 'I saw his snarl coming down the path towards me.' Clifton wrote his story 'The blue sky sits in the sun and so do I.' Allan's,

THE FISH SWIM

The fish swim in the sea
And when I eat them
They swim in my throat.

Allan's, *The Sparrow*: 'The sparrow sits on our clothes line and I pick up a stone and hit his bones.'

Mary's, *Day*: 'The day is a beginner day, only I went to bed before he did.'

'The willows are falling all the time,' said Eric.
'Let's go butter-cupping,' said Stuart.
'The idgy-bidgies cried when it rained,' wrote Ted.

Most of these sayings, whether poetic or not, came from young children, and I felt that statements such as these undoubtedly are heard quite commonly by mothers before children come to school. Such phrases, and sentences were collected and set aside with the lino prints on a wall where the better things were kept. (Chapter 14.) As other perceptive statements and poems were heard and written, they too were added to the list. This was the beginning of real poetry. However at this stage I did not differentiate between poetry and prose. I found then that after we had decided that these statements were more sincere than the others we were able to progress. It is essential to creative teaching that the better elements be selected by all the class and that we try to involve all in the decisions, for no progress can be made in values or expression without this. It is evident that certain children will at times make advances in their creative expression, but unless we are aware of these happenings the work is valueless except to the child concerned. Much of this book rests upon the recognition of these advances and the establishment of class sets of values.

DANCING

With tipping toes she goes
Up,

44

One hand down and one hand up
And not a sound she makes.

KELVIN

Kelvin's *Dancing* had come a long way from Leslie's thrush poem.

THE TYRE

See the tyre go higher
and higher
Fffffffff-ffffffff
And see it go higher and higher and higher,
Fffffffff-ffffffff

MARY, 7 years

I noticed that alliteration and assonance came naturally to the children, and I suspected that they had a well developed feeling for speech rhythms. I saw that most of the children would be unlikely to make very great progress in this work, so I decided to depart from my earlier decision not to meddle with the development that was taking place. I felt that these older children could quite probably benefit from a series of short lessons in which I would extend their confidence to express themselves through imagery of their own making. The exercises took the form of describing happenings and observations in the course of work on one of the nature topics. The older pupils needed a deeper feeling of freedom in their thinking, something more akin to that of the infant groups.

I have always felt that any contribution by myself at such times was likely to be unsuccessful in the first

instance. I was prepared to accept this, for I knew that the freedom of usage of such figures of speech that children commonly use would probably come afterwards. I used a good deal of adult poetic imagery to assist this lesson development. I had been assured that an infant's speech was far in advance in its feeling, and I considered that I was not damaging the older children by engaging them in this series of lessons. The lessons were continued for a few weeks, and there came out of it a good deal of contrived but some quite poetic and beautiful writings as well: 'the willow combed his fingers in the tidal waters', 'I heard the dark in the cry of the morepork', 'splinters of fish in the light', and 'the poplar was a cage full of sparrows'.

There appeared to be a parallel between this stage of development and that through which we had worked in pottery. The potters who had the benefit of continued growth from their beginning at the school developed in their technical ability and knowledge continuously and naturally, but those who came later took time to absorb the values of the establishing group. It was reasonably easy for late comers, or in this case the older children, to absorb the feeling and values for pottery and lino work but it was a different matter in language. Idiom was as yet little appreciated. The wall display of paintings and lino blocks and the pottery collection provided satisfactory influences in the arts and crafts, and the collection of poems and 'sayings' was the beginning of the growth of language values.

45

Morepork, David W., 12 years

Tree and birds by Bevin

All work was presented in some way or other to the whole class, and a basis of values was developed, so that through the process of discussion and assessment a piece of prose or poetry was recognised as being of value or not. In consequence a piece of writing under examination was always considered somewhat dispassionately. There was no place for disagreement with the opinion of the majority because of a temporary dislike of the author, nor was there a place for unworthy praise of poor work.

Even though most children discussed the work and said whether they liked or disliked an expression, they showed clearly that their statement was based on values of good personal judgement.

Now and then it was sad to see a child present to the group something that he attached particular importance to and then find that the other children could not agree that it was very good. Occasionally a child would put one of his own paintings up on the wall without the permission of the group. On the other hand the children showed much interest and consideration of individual standards. They were kind to children who rarely shone in their expression and saw that what was 'good' for one person was not the same 'good' for another. Although it was possible for any of the children to write work of the highest order the frequency with which they did this varied greatly. A creative approach to learning does allow the child to reach points of great satisfaction, but when efforts were not of that measure children were tolerant enough to accept with favour what was average but of great personal effort. The comment, 'That is very good for Colin' was not condescension. For they knew that they themselves might at any time produce writing that was very ordinary.

Soon many had begun to select their own subjects, and these children rarely required stimulation (see Joyce's writing, page 48) but there were those who could not actively engage themselves with the freedom of forty or fifty minutes daily. There were some who for long periods of time did not write anything that was considered to be of value. I felt that I had to increase the amount of environmental study so that there was sufficient stimulation.

I drew their attention more and more to things such as the passing weather, the changing of the habits of birds and animals, and our interaction with our environment. It was necessary to induce attitudes of awareness (see Chapter 9) in the children so that they became observers as well as appreciators of the world around them.

Early one morning when the starlings began to chatter more loudly than usual three children went out to investigate, and they found the plumbers clearing out various nests from the spouting and roofing iron. They collected the young birds in their nests and took them to a large hollow post where they 're-arranged' them. Some of the mother birds came back to them, and one mother bird continued to look after her nest, but the others were abandoned. We thought this was most unusual.

The circumstances led the children to a good deal of writing and some painting and lino print work. Rosalie wrote about the mother birds, 'The pretty bird creeps on the tree nicely, softly and soundlessly.'

BIRDS
The birds are only little now. They are not old enough to be kicked out so they are still there. The birds are very bad because they pinch my straw to make their nests of.

NELL

STARLINGS
The birds are awful things; they screech and scratch all day long. Their yellow beaks are as big as their bellies and they swallow huge worms in a disgusting way.

TREVOR, 12 years

Starling baby by Joyce

47

Starling by Rosalie

Other children joined the activity and wrote reports and poems. We isolated phrases and images such as these:

'Soon they will have feathers, shining bluish-black.'
'They feel funny when I touch them.'
'The mother has worms in her throat.'
'We saw their fringy tails and the hairs on their bellies.'
'Squawking in ragged nests.'

MY BROTHER

'One wet wintery morning I set out for the store. My brother was sick so I had to go quickly. It was not raining when I left, but I hadn't gone more than a mile when there came a sudden downpour.

'Quickly I found a sheltered place under some trees and there I sat wondering when the rain would stop. A few minutes after when the rain had not stopped I began to get worried. Would my brother get worse; would they get worried about me? What if they came to look for me and could not find me in this sheltered place? All these things flashed through my mind. I straightened myself and thought 'I am going to get out of this place and hurry and get the medicine.' But the rain was falling so heavily and the wind was blowing so strongly that I almost lost my feet. Again I crawled under the shelter.

'I began to hate this spot and to think it had been the cause of all this trouble; then much to my joy all of a sudden it cleared up. I jumped up and left that place, vowing I would never go there again . . .'

JOYCE, 11 years

NIGHT TIME

It was a pitch black night.
A night of misfortune;
A night of getting nowhere;
A night of running into things.

I put my hand out, it touched something unseen.
A shock of fear went through me.
The fear had almost stopped my heart.
I peered with fear into the darkness,
And there in front of me were bulls
Bulls with horns so big and tough.
Then with frightened yells and screams
And forgetting all past fears
I tore back and without stopping, entered
the gate and ran to the yard . . .

4

THE DEVELOPMENT OF THE CRAFTS

THE first efforts to model figures were never very good, so in the four to five years following the beginning of pottery not very much figure work was done. I know that part of the cause for this was my own influence, in that I was conscious of the technical difficulties of firing very thick clay and discouraged thick pottery. We had not yet developed hollow-figure work. Now and then one of the older children made a group or single clay-figure, and occasionally I could see what had stimulated this. Once or twice Varley modelled figures and objects related to a poem we had read, and sometimes Kelvin or Bevin made an animal that was related to some actual observation, but they and the other children did not at first associate figure-making with actual experiences. More often someone would say spontaneously, 'I think I will make a seal,' or 'I could make a kangaroo.'

This chapter is about developments that took place over a period of nearly three years. I believe that the final success of most of this work came from the forging of a close association of the child's thinking with some actual experience or observation. This was true for all of the advances made in lino cutting, fabric printing, and wood block printing and carving. It began one day when we were doing an English lesson.

Although every window was open the room was oppressively hot, and the children's attention wandered. I had decided to give this lesson because I had noted that nearly all the children had need for this particular information. It was very rare that I had to teach the whole class together; usually I would be engaged with small groups. I had been in the habit of making notes on children's language needs. These I recorded on individual cards so that at any time I could consider a particular child and see what lessons he needed in language. Generally I grouped together those with the same needs. Every day I taught lessons such as these or organized small groups for developmental work that was related less to deficiencies in grammar than to those in expression.

I called the children's attention often to the task in hand without much success, when I saw a stranger walking up the school drive towards the drinking fountain.

He had a small billy in his hand, and I saw that he was about to fill it and go, without asking permission. Ron and David, who I suspected hadn't been with me during the lesson, caught my eye as I looked out of the window and they saw the visitor too. These boys were as much respectors of other people's property as most youngsters, and I was surprised that they drew my attention to this 'trespasser' in rather a carping way. I wasn't concerned that this person or any person for that matter should help himself to the water. I felt that he showed good sense in not disturbing me, and as I tapped the blackboard to draw the children's attention again I thought that I would explain the happening to everyone after the lesson was over. I ignored both the stranger, then fast disappearing down the drive and the two boys, Ron and David . . . But, they had their say.

'Pardon me, sir, but I don't think you realise what is going on out there,' said Ron.

'He saw all right, I saw him look,' added David.

I stopped at this interruption, and looked indulgently at the two boys, and wondered if I would be able to regain even the amount of attention I had before these first remarks.

'Too right he saw! Didn't you, sir?' said one of them.

'Saw whom, when, where?' asked Barbara, who was now looking out the window nearly too late to see the departing stranger.

'There he is! There he is! Can we go after him and catch him?' shouted Martha.

When all the fuss was over, several of the children looked surprised and disappointed, for they had not seen him.

'See what?' said Colin. 'I never seen anyone.'

'Who was it?' asked Mavis. But he was gone and with him went my lesson on the use of the verb 'to see'. Ron and David remained indignant, and many others were excited and had begun to discuss the stranger.

This sort of thing can be very trying when the teacher has a definite aim in view, and this lesson was one in which the object *was* definite. I was a little annoyed that the interruption had come at that time and wondered if I should attempt to drag the class together and try to complete the lesson. Then I saw that I might be able to make another lesson out of this happening.

'What did he look like, Martha?' asked Eric and Raymond together. I supposed they asked her because she had made so much noise about the man. Her description was well out.

'He had blue dungarees on and a ripped shirt, a brown one. And yes, he had black hair . . . or it looked blackish,' she said.

'I'm sure he didn't. His hair might have been darkish, but his shirt was a tan colour and I never saw any rips.'

'Yes, but I know who it was,' said David, 'I saw him on a bike with a shovel the other day. That chap has black wavy hair and blue longs.'

'But he may not have been the same man.'

'I think you're all wrong,' butted in Alma. 'None of

us have really seen this man before, and those who really saw him just now will agree, won't you Ron?'

This was the beginning of something new. In small groups everyone had a chance to have their say about his appearance and speculated on how he came to this isolated valley. We heard descriptions, and saw that they were still many and varied and that there was a need to record a description of him. Some wrote 'Wanted' notices, while others wrote simple but rather tedious descriptions of the man.

We were reading Hemingway's *The Old Man and the Sea* at that time, so I went back to the first pages and re-read the section in which he describes the old man. I found myself still reading after ten pages and was able to indicate that the description was still going on, with the story, even on the last page. Many of the children then attempted to write a story in which they involved the description of our man.

When the afternoon came, many went on and repeated their accounts in their own language-writing option time, but then other work began. Brett was reading his book, examining the description of the characters, and Barbara and Mary were looking into their library books too. I organized a discussion on the way authors introduce character descriptions. David I. called this 'the dullest part of the book'.

The work so far had included general and rather ordinary teaching, but the quality of the observations and attention was extremely good. The verb 'to see' remained untaught. The moment had been 'right' for this sort of work, and I am sure that any attempt to synthesize these conditions would have failed.

'Tiger', one of the Davids, had found the verbal work rather difficult, particularly relating the description to a story beginning. He came to me and asked if he could 'do his description in clay'. He assured me that he could show me exactly what the man was like. He looked at me for a second or two, and in case I should say no, he said he could rearrange his day a bit and do the description after he had done the clay figure. Again a moment had arrived when I might have made an

David ('Tiger') modelling a head

Two heads by David ('Tiger')

Head by Brett

error, but that I didn't (I am sure I made many many such errors in this school) was due to Tiger's enthusiasm.

He rolled a ball of red clay into a good consistency and soon was fingering out a good-sized head. He promised to return to the verbal description after, and he said, full of promises, he would give a talk about his head too. This led others to start a head after the description was finished. Stories came in with some more accurate descriptions and one or two comments on character introductions from books of fiction. Recommendations from groups of those accounts that were to be read aloud came to me, and those who were already making figures rested their elbows or wrists over the edges of the work bench and rubbed the drying clay from between their fingers and listened as I read.

Twenty or so clay busts and figures lay drying, all in guarded places (for the work was of the highest order)

52

Left to right, heads by Valerie, Martha, Jennifer and Ron

around the room. Carefully we gouged out the inside of the heads so that the clay would fire without bursting, a solution so simple that I wondered why we hadn't thought of it before. The heads were all different and I smiled to myself, for not one of them looked like the the visitor with the billy. I didn't expect them to, though. This reminded me of the pots envisaged on paper and the very different ones that were actually made. I knew that this was the same sort of departure, and any attempt to relate the clay descriptions (if they were, in any case, descriptions) to the verbal one would be inadvisable.

'Tiger' delivered his short talk and admitted that he had started to make the man but in the end had liked what he did so much that he left it that way.

This sort of work in modelling had been attempted before, but never in circumstances such as this to stimulate interest and a need for creative outlets. Thus there had never been the satisfaction that comes out of experience. I feel that this is one of the reasons why work of quality is so hard to get from children. The figures delighted every child, and the modelling went on and on. Each figure was discussed as it was completed, in the same way as the poetry and lino prints were. The satisfaction continued for a time, until a day came when five poor and incomplete heads and figures were done and the whole activity stopped. It was one of those spiritless end-of-the-week Fridays, when creative work (and surely formal lessons too) should have been abandoned in favour of some relaxing occupations. Three of these heads were finished, but the activity in figure making didn't continue in the same spirit as it had arisen.

Ron had been reading a story about natives who ornamented themselves with shells and bone nose-skewers, and he produced his head, which was based on

53

Large head by David W.

the strange visitor. His sister Jennifer also made two native heads. In many ways their work was like the very first work done by 'Tiger'. I have often felt that children may be held back in creative expression such as this through some lack of extension to their work. Jennifer and Ron extended the work further. I saw that the children had recognised the need to extend themselves. Ron and Jenny's native figures indicated this.

Some fifty heads were fired in the kiln, and after the third firing we saw that the shelves would have to be culled of the weaker ones so that the best could be displayed.

Some time later, almost a year after, while in the midst of a study of a tribe of New Guinea natives from a set of short stories we were reading, a number of children recalled the terra-cotta heads and asked to do some more. This time they wanted to make very large ones that could be part of the room décor while the study went on. The solid method of building heads would not be suitable, and while I debated in my mind the desirability or necessity of introducing full sculptural methods to them, one of the boys suggested that coiling would be a good way to make them if the maker remembered the correct place at which to expand or contract the figure.

'Anyway, we could stick some clay on to the shaped head, couldn't we?' We tried this out.

On a coiled base coil after coil was added to build up the neck, and then it was expanded slowly to make the chin, the lips, sometimes an open mouth, out again

Heads by **Sonny**, left, and Eric

David modelling, and elephant by Ngaire, 12 years

for the nose, and so on. Many were made, and usually they had open heads and became known as 'decapitated pakehas'. Mouths were carved out, and eyes and ears were poked through into the interior so that when they were fired small smudge fires could be lit in them that would 'breathe' smoke. These orifices were even given curved lips inside to catch smoke as it rose.

In much the same way Eric and David and others made animals of some size. To the coiled body-shapes they added legs and coiled or solid heads, and if fate was kind they stuck. They were rested on their four feet until they became drier and then were decorated.

A certain amount of small figure making engaged the children over the last year in which I was at Oruaiti. We fired these with the very efficient salt-glaze kiln that we had built a year previously.

*　　　*　　　*

Rhinoceros, Eric, 11 years

Much of the first work in paint, lino cutting, and printing concerned such things as trees, birds, houses, or people, and often as not they were done as the simple statement of the one thing. For example, Owen's cut of a tree (page 37) and Joyce's *Starling* (page 47) were 'alone', and there is no reference to other social or environmental things. This was due, I think, to the attention we were giving to one subject after another. It was the first indication that it is better to study one subject deeply rather than many superficially. Each of these topics had been well studied.

Whereas lino cutting seemed an adequate medium for certain expression, it did not seem very suitable for the very small things the children were recognising as 'good shapes' and 'good textures' in other nature work. Such things as the seeds of plants, the insides of flowers, the spore structure of ferns, the legs of flies, growing seedlings, and the tissues of plants and animals, all of which have great beauty, seemed to have a quality that made them valuable for design rather than things which stood by themselves.

I purchased a low-powered microscope that gave a wide field of about X10 magnifications, and with this instrument it was possible to have a large number of growing seeds within the field. This microscope added great possibilities to nature study and brought within our range of experience almost anything that the children observed. We found, too, that the beauties of small seeds and insects were most startling. For instance, the seeds of vervain were found to be extremely beautiful.

Drawing of designs from these observations became just as much a part of nature work as the writing of

Water buffalo by Eric

Bull by Eric

poetry did at a later time. Now and then one of these designs became used as a lino design. E. C. Seelye, who had specialized knowledge of the techniques of design and fabric printing, spent two days in the school and introduced us to the techniques of designing and printing fabrics with large lino blocks and fabric screens. Dick gathered about him seven of the older children who had trees, birds, and roosters in mind from the previous day's work. Peering through the gaps was Allan, who was then a very small but interested boy. He watched Trevor painting and designing in shellac directly on to a silk screen. Dick went on to Joyce and encouraged her further with her *Pumpkin Tissue* lino block, which was nearly ready to print. Allan in the meantime had picked up a large brush and sat beside Trevor.

'Can I use this one?' he asked.

'Better ask,' was Trevor's reply as he went on carefully sketching in his design in chalk.

'Of. course you may,' said Dick, 'and here's a screen for you, but will you know what to do and will you be careful?'

'I was watching,' he said. In ten minutes Allan had finished, even before I realised that he had started. This was his first fabric screen, which he based on nature work.

Large cut-paper stencil screen printing was introduced to the small children. As well lino blocks, now large and worked with even larger gouges, were used.

Allan screen printing

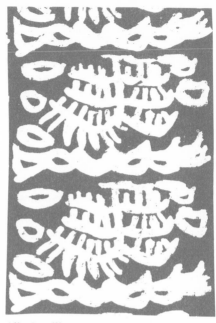

Allan's willow pattern

Barbara and Allan cutting lino

These fabrics were put to immediate use by the children in sewing class for aprons and pinafores. Some were used for curtains in the classroom and for cushion covers at home.

I felt that the use and display of these fabrics was again an integral part of the process of establishing atmosphere for creative things in the room. At the same time Mr Seelye introduced us to negative screen processes, and a great wealth of fabrics sprang out of the confidence this skill gave us.

Although fabric screen work was used mainly for work with the microscope, a host of subjects was used by the children: *Fish* by Sonny, *Roosters* by David, *Wild Carrot Seed* by Anna, *Crab* by Irene, *Beetle* by Eliza,

59

and *Butterfly* by Sonny were a few. Trees and birds and especially fish seemed to be the favourite subjects, and again each was complete in itself, usually in one colour, but at times another colour was brushed on top for certain detail, e.g. *Butterfly*, which was typical of many produced by Miss F.'s class.

Gradually more and more ideas were taken from the individual studies that were going on, and multiple colour screens were done. The designing did not go past the stage of a unit in repeat. Textural effects were rarely used, but when they were the textural effect was usually the final touch rather than the basis of the whole design.

Joyce, Nell and fabric.

Shark design, Owen

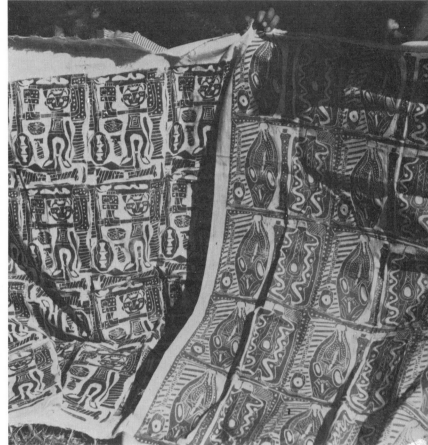

Left, caterpillar design by Brett

Below, 'Taboo' native design and bottle design by David H.

Lino blocks continued to be done, but only rarely did a child design one especially for a fabric. David H.'s *Bottle Design* and *Taboo* indicate an individual's personal preference for lino printed fabrics.

Nature study supplied most of the ideas for fabrics: *Nautilus* by Joyce, *Shark* by Owen, and *Bird* by Barbara.

I noted that the more intellectual children used more abstract design, for example Brett's *Caterpillar on a Leaf*. One of the most involved designs was David H.'s

61

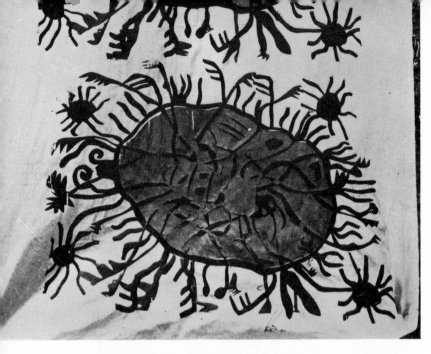

Drosera Fly-catcher, a three-colour fabric print in which 'the tongues of the plant are trying to lick the flies into its arms'.

As lino cutting and fabric screen printing became more familiar the size of the prints became larger, and I noted that the children were at last stating a whole situation particularly in the lino work. Roosters were fighting with each other with people watching and hens and rats about, three horsemen were droving around a cliff, two people were cooking out of doors on a barbecue stove and there was long grass with caterpillars and birds on it. No longer were birds cut without their homes or some sort of environment, but subjects such as trees became treated in design unlike the somewhat stark manner of the past.

Drosera Fly-catcher by David H.

Fallen tree by Kenneth   Bitch and hare by Dennis

The development of clay was proceeding meanwhile. At that time oil painting was being introduced, for we saw the need for a paint to be stiffer so that textural effects could be worked more effectively. Colour could be applied on top of other colour, and many of the pottery techniques would present themselves naturally: scraping through colour to base, combing with card combs and brushes, sticks and bunches of wire. A number of textural surfaces were collected, such as bark,

seeds, sands, gravel, leaves, petals, and feathers. As well, man-made textures were then coming to our notice: wire netting, rubber soles, sand-papers, paint brush marks, fabrics of all kinds, and papers and leathers of many surfaces. Clay pressings of some of these were used now and then by some children.

'Look at this pattern of a sea-egg shell on clay. Good isn't it?'

'Let's print a bit of wire netting on a bit.'

'Or this leaf would print nicely too.' Actual ink printings off leaves occupied the children for one nature study art period one day. They did not do any more.

Allan decorating pressed tile with coloured slips

This work led the children to see that it would be a valuable experience to print lino-blocks on to clay surfaces. At the same time as this awareness of the quality of textural surfaces began, I observed its effect on the thinking of some of them.

'I saw the clouds printed over the paddocks.'

Irene building up a plaque

Irene decorating a plaque

Bird plaque by Jennifer

Bees, plaque by Mary

'Seagulls' feet printed over the paddocks.'
'Forked footprints of seagulls dying on the beach.'
'The horses' textured trot.'

The lino blocks were pressed very firmly into tile press moulds. For a time all the children did this sort of work, but soon they tired of it and only now and then did someone do one. Their interest changed to bas relief plaque and tile making.

A close link was seen between a number of processes: the cutting of lino and the same process of cutting into clay, the printing of a lino block into clay for a reverse (or positive) of the incision process, the incision into

Tree by David W.

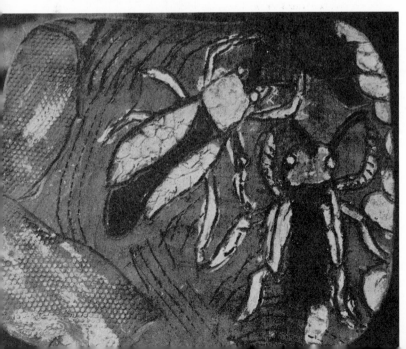

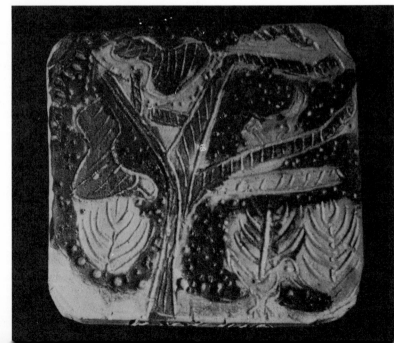

clay, and the relief building up of clay. These skills had their influence on the others and gave satisfactions of a particular kind, and as the children worked at each they needed at times to go on to another of the group for added satisfaction. Clay relief work allowed for decoration with many-coloured slips, and this led a child to see that a lino block could be decorated by hand with a number of coloured inks and printed.

Then it was not a very great step to tint a dry print with water dyes. Dyeing with coloured water-soluble dyes became a regular part of all lino print work, and the children found that the density and selection of colour gave added experience and added interest to the print. A print that wasn't quite 'right' in one colour was often made very creditable when tinted with dyes.

I noted that like Irene many people built up their plaques in a linial way, much as they cut their lino-blocks. Then they fill in the lined-up picture. Mary, her sister, used a textural surface as part of the means of building up her picture. This did not have any raised surfaces.

The children in Miss F.'s classes, who had not so much lino cutting experience and who were all very impressed with the relief building process, were very different in their attack when they approached the task themselves. They built up the tiles and plaques in solid form and added texture where it was needed.

In the end all these techniques were used by the children. I saw that the use of the form of building up of a tile was now more clearly related to the needs, as dictated by the subject. Jennifer's *Trees* and *Birds* were very lightly glazed to bring out the best ceramic colours.

Cardboard mobile masks had been decorated with colour and textural surface materials such as sand and sawdust and had been hung on forked branches for some time. Then I suggested that since we could press-mould pots into free forms in plaster moulds we could press-mould masks also. We were studying New Guinea then, and mask making would add to our craft experiences.

Master shapes were made and moulds were poured. Pressings were made and decorated from these. Again the children could cut out eyes, mouths, and ears. Later very large moulds were made and from these a great number of basically similar masks were made. It was a natural extension to free mask-making in clay . . .

David had taken a piece of planed box-wood many years ago when he was a 'primer' and had made the first wood-cut of a 'man shape'. Later, others used wood for blocks, and this led to relief cutting in wood as well as in lino. I was not surprised to see the children using lino in preference to wood, for it allowed almost all the experience that wood offered at many times the speed. Still, there is satisfaction in a sharp chisel or gouge used well, and many knew this. After clay pressings were well under way I introduced the gouges and chisels again and began to make a large mask on my own account. New Guinea work had led us to a study of masks generally, and my mask was somewhat like an African

Press-moulding of masks
A pressed mask

68

one. I continued, and soon found that Eric, Kenneth and David, and Walter wanted to make them too. Raymond began a boat, and I recalled our beginnings. Several wooden masks were carved during two terms.

I found that one of the best ways of starting off a new technique such as wood carving was to start to make something for myself. Very soon I would have as many as genuinely wanted to work in that material. I began the making of small ceramic brooches in the same way.

Oil painting gradually enveloped other media, to advantage. Crayons, chalk, pastel, sand, and glue were used with oil to added effect.

Sarah's *Three People* and David's *Roosters* were painted on large surfaces, four to five feet long and as wide, and this alone added much to the style of painting.

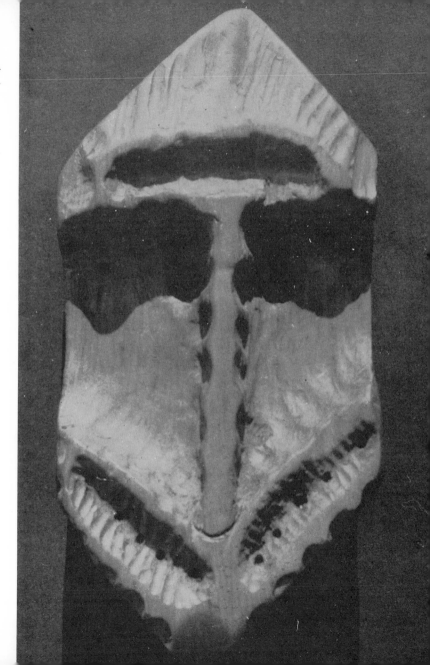

Masks, left by David I., right by Eric

5

THE DEVELOPMENT OF LANGUAGE EXPRESSION

THE starlings became important to the children and filled their thoughts and they developed strong feelings about them. The children wrote about them, painted pictures and did lino cuts. All this expressive work was part of the study, and through it they came to see starlings as creatures with feelings of their own. The children, as it were, felt with them.

The clearing out of the nests from the guttering involved us in an increasingly deep study of the subject. Almost every day there was some writing by most children about their observations. At this time most of the day's work was still quite formal, but we found that we could use about two hours a day for nature study. Some of this was used for teaching and actual observation of habits of the birds concerned, but as the detail was built up we used more and more of this period for expression. I saw that the amount of work that the children presented to me often bore little relationship to the time that it took to produce it. Sometimes a small lino block did not seem to involve much work, but I saw that the brevity of the statement was the important thing about the work. I saw, too, that even the short piece of writing that was not very well thought out should be accepted, for often the same subject came up again, and as the writers became able to deal with it they produced new and more complete statements. These were not revisions of the old; they were new attacks on the material and seemed to be unconnected with the earlier statements.

I found that I had to have faith in the expressive part of the work, for when I did the children invariably would excel when I least expected it. I saw that there were intense satisfactions to be got from such a study of a topic. We could find opportunities for all sorts of good expressive work in several 'subjects' as I called them then. I called this 'integration of expression'. I came to conclude that this procedure was much more effective than any I had used in the past to educate the children. From that time the deep and intense study of a topic became the most important characteristic of our school work, but as time went on I found that such

Mask by David W.

Night faces by Clifton

studies need not be carried out by the whole class at once: children could follow studies of their own personal interests, though those in turn often involved other children.

This topic-centred activity occupied us in subject after subject, until I found that most of the day was occupied by it. I found that I still had to have definite times for the formal subjects, and there had to be times when we stopped individual work and came together for social activities such as singing and music making. I planned lessons frequently throughout the day, but I allowed time for the children to engage themselves in more and more personal investigation and expression. I saw that on some days I taught too much and occupied the time so much that little expressive work resulted. On the others I taught too little, and I saw that some children were in need of further direction or teaching. I began to record individual language needs then, and gave regular lessons where I saw that they would be helpful. I saw fit to give any lesson that I felt would assist the enthusiasm and accuracy of the expression.

I never related a lesson on a topic such as the use of 'there' and 'there's' to the actual work done in creative writing. At certain times, when the children were writing accounts that I had requested for some special reason, I saw that I could and should require the papers to be discussed with another pupil or myself so that they might develop an awareness for form and error. I have never found that this thoughtful study of form in practical writing reduces the flow of the creative expression.

At the beginning of my attempts to bring out creative thinking I was worried because the work appeared so much poorer than the writings the children had produced when I was using formal methods of teaching. But after only a few weeks I felt sure that the more creative methods produced better work than I could have obtained from a more formal approach. The informal creative writing is the measure of the writer's real ability, and I thought that the criticism and encouragement of this was more likely to be related to the individual's growth than set lessons. For example, Martha was reading an unfinished story as part of a report on hawks: 'When we went to Waimahana we had to walk all the way. At Roy's farm there were lots of sheep and lambs about. Suddenly we saw a hawk gliding about looking for rotten sheep. We walked up the hill and down to Waimahana and when we were half way up we saw some wool on the track.' Completing her story she joined Allan, David W., Rosy, and Jennifer to discuss hawks, which were a pest in this valley.

Allan read out his story: 'A hawk was flying over the green hills and a poor old sheep was dying below with his eyes pecked out; I hate to see the cruel old hawk laughing above at the sheep.'

Like Martha he added to the discussion with stories of his own and his father's experiences, which were far too long and involved to be written down. Some of their oral accounts in this group discussion surpassed what they had written down, especially in their odd statements and child-like ways of simplifying. Rosalie's story about the hawk 'flying on one wing' was the sort of thing that I was pleased to see others appreciated, for it had the same clarity of expression that I recognised from the stories the children were telling each other.

Jennifer wrote about seeing a hawk from the barn window and 'opening the door like a whispering sound'. In all stories there appeared to be a working out of ideas and experiences rather than the writing of a specific story or poem. This working out of ideas was more characteristic of certain children, such as David W. 'As the hawks glide side by side, their wings look raw, I don't know why . . . I know why. It's because he's high up in the air. I can see two of their heads looking down on us with their curved beaks looking down too, to see if I am going to shoot at them.'

This piece of work had engaged a few children for about two hours, and such had been the interest of the others that in the afternoon all the stories were read out and I gave a short lesson on hawks in our swamps and about farms and hawks. We also discussed Allan's lino print, *The Hawk and the Sheep*.

As can be seen, the writing tended to persist around a particular topic until interest had been satisfied. In many instances the interest began with an actual experience. David's short story really happened, and this story and his discussion on hawks helped other children who were

Hawk and sheep, Allan, 10 years

in search of a topic to write and talk about. Interest was not always immediate, but tended to build up over a few weeks, as did the amount of work done. Our system of short lessons and talks helped those who then wanted to write and talk and to do so informally. Free time for writing is still the most requested period at the day's planning time.

Looking back after ten years at what was happening in language development and expression, I realise that there was much cause for satisfaction; almost without exception the children were writing, reading, thinking, and talking about things they knew in their environment and in which they were genuinely interested. The short lessons I gave were always popular, but I noticed that the information in them was rarely used directly in the stories told or written by the children. Rather did my lessons remind children of facets of their experience which they would have otherwise missed in their telling and writing.

The amount each child wrote was small at this stage. The chief virtue of stories like David's was sincerity and originality of thought, and this was what I praised; but even this often hung merely on one or two perceptive statements. David, Martha, Dennis, Derek, and the others appeared to write in a characteristic style, and it would seem reasonable to hope that this individual quality would be retained and would give pleasure to themselves and their friends. Here are a number of stories that seemed to point in this direction.

BROKEN SHELLS

'When I was walking along I saw lots of shells with their noises broken and their tails right off. I picked up one by the noise and carried it to the water where it broke to pieces.'

MAVIS, 9 years

OUR SWING

'On Saturday afternoon Colin and I went over to have a swing on the tree. When we got there, there was no swing, so we went around the tree to see if there was a swing. It was lying dead on the ground. I picked it up and tied it around the branch, then I got up and had a swing. Plonk on the ground I fell.'

MAVIS

CAKES

'When Mum bakes cakes I watch her, but when she gets mad at me she tells me to set the table so she can get rid of me for a while. If I finish before her she tells me to go to play and I feel mad at Mum because I have to go to play. The one thing I like is watching Mum bake cakes. I don't know why but I do.'

BARBARA, 8 years

The elements of simple perception in these stories usually highlight ordinary happenings, but Barbara's story is more. It is an example of a sincere type of expression, in this case of frustration, that appeared more and more commonly as the children accepted the freedom to write as they felt.

The children admired these stories and their own kind of thinking. In the same way, later, after we had talked about chants and tried to use the chant as a mode of expression they realised that they had been accustomed to chant (some would say 'sing song') their thoughts as they walked alone on their rounds or over their farms, and they came to regard chanting as their natural form of musical expression and enjoyed it all the more for that reason.

The wide range of writings done was in most cases coupled with some form of illustrative expression in the arts. This does not mean that the writing was considered to be the more important expression nor that the illustration was an afterthought. David was the initiator of all the work on hawks, but he wrote his few comments at the end. His mime dance of two hawks was far more important to him. I saw that some children, such as Derek and Mike, consistently did work that we all admired and commended, and this work was mainly painting. During discussions that we had on the set of hawk paintings, on the mime dance, the poetry, and the prose writings, Derek observed that often he painted things that he didn't mention in his story. In many cases children expressed their thoughts and apperceptions in visual art or drama before they did so in words.

Other children remarked that painting was an opportunity to reconsider thoughts or even go back to the original experience and that this allowed them to realise their purposes more clearly.

This led to the suggestion to paint 'the things you didn't say so much about in the story'. Of course in practice this didn't imply a complete break in activity for what the child is really doing is reconsidering the criteria and finding certain things 'unsaid'. It just happens that a good deal of such work appears entirely new.

Children like Allan continued to write in a simple way to convey their thoughts, but they gradually developed their abilities in illustrative expressive work. Thus they expanded their thoughts in a natural way and filled out the inadequacies of their writings. Time has shown that some of these children did not develop their abilities in creative writing much beyond simple sincere stories. However, because of the new developments in the arts, especially with Maori children, a strong development was seen in language. As well the children came to accept the idea that the set of expressions, such as the story about the hawk or the pukeko, the lino blocks, the discussions, and the paintings, should all be considered *as a whole*. For example, it would not have been right to assess only Allan's rather immature stumbling after words and fail to recognize his better lino print or his talk on the birds that live on one of his father's farms.

This assessment *in wholes* by the children, and the individual way in which they liked to work, should be understood and encouraged. It requires sensitivity to varying situations and the ability to recognise the best time to urge a child to go on to a better and fuller expression.

This is especially true of children like Allan, who seek a modicum of satisfaction in creative writing without a great deal of success (and it is to be remembered that Allan was a child who began by making good oral statements). Their lack of success becomes apparent to them when they hear the fuller and more expressive statements read out by the others. If these children are encouraged to make statements in some other medium, such as painting, pottery, or drama, they are able to express themselves satisfactorily. The final result may be a part in a drama, a series of paintings about the subject, and half a page of simple story. The little writing Allan did here, his descriptions of experiences without regard to what he had written, his lino print, and his comment on other work was a *whole* that the children accepted as most creditable.

PUKEKOS

'Nobody knows where the pukeko goes on his long
    yellow legs,
With a head on one end and a tail on the other.
Their legs are long and their beaks are short.
His colour's bright and his tail's white.
He is not dark, he's a very dark blue.
He looks black, but he's a nice pukeko blue.
Guess where he lives?
Down in the bull paddock.
He's so noisy he gets on my nerves.

VALERIE

Pukeko birds by Mary M.

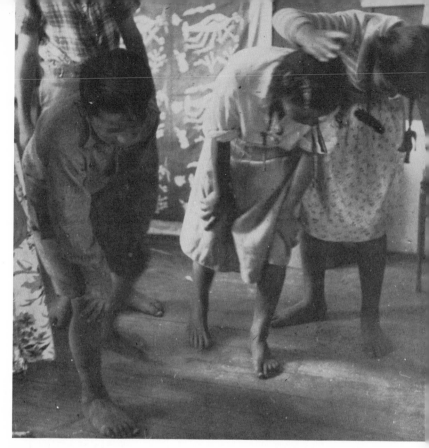

PUKEKO

'As they proudly strut they go caa, caa, softer, softer and softer and at last they fly up into the weeping willows and give their last caa, caa and go to sleep.

'Bang, bang, out comes Herbert with a gun. He sees me and sings out, "Want a pukeko?" I say, "Yep" and he throws one over. I sing out, "Pretty fat eh?" "Too right!"

'After he went away I caught two kahawai and put the pukeko in a different bag and went home and had a good feed of pukeko and fish and not to be greedy, I gave some to granny.'

VALERIE

Mary lives close to the pukeko nests and the swamp that is their home. Her lino print, and Valerie's first poem, were only part of the general run of stories at that time. Stories, art, and drama arose from pukeko observations just as they had when the children were watching hawks. In this case the interest was kept to observations by the river and a nest Clifton found. Daily the young chicks were visited, and the birds, in a way pukekos have, became quite used to our incautious looking. Factual reports were written as a science project, and the climax to this piece of study was a pukeko poem and its dramatization into a dance mime.

Environmental subjects such as this were inclined to build up a state of expression in the school with a number of beginnings for child interest. Sometimes this remained individual or was shared by one other child.

The pukeko dance mime

In the case of the hawk study nearly all made some expressive statement.

The Kiwi by Michael and *Early Birds* by Mary, the two following pieces of writing, resulted when these

77

two children came together for criticism and extension of their interest in birds. The group of two, I found was often the most effective kind of grouping.

Some of the children were engaged in the communication of fact or information during this time. Thus David and Allan and their friends discussed hawks and trapping them. They made traps from simple materials and explained the use of rat traps to kill them. Others were investigating hen rings and ages of hens, hen-houses and pigeon lofts, but Michael and Mary were really engaged in communicating feeling.

EARLY BIRDS

'Early birds catch the first worm; I don't know why but they do. When it is rainy they would not catch the first worm, but they would try and that makes the day fine.

'I do not know why the early bird gets up early. I have a little kitten and she gets up early and she catches the first bird. I know something about birds that get up early, they do that because they want to catch the first, first, worm.

'The bird wakes me up for school, but the bird that gets up first is a sparrow, but thrushes and all sorts of birds get up early too.

'I get up early because I have to go to school, but the bird that catches the first worm, always washes his eyes earlier, before the worm gets under the ground. The early birds are really fast, because then they hear the rooster, they will be up so they can beat the rooster to the worms.'

MARY

THE KIWI

'A few years ago Wilfred found a middle-sized kiwi around by a puriri tree at Waimahana. After a few hours they caught it and brought it back on the horse. Mum tied its leg to a string and the other end she chained to the pohutukawa tree which is just outside our house.

'A few months later it got used to us so we let it go and it snoozed around the house after worms and snails and crumbs. For a while the dogs hated it but after a while they were the best of friends.

'One day when we were at the table having lunch the kiwi came into the house and jumped up on the chair as if to say have something to eat? We all laughed and laughed at that bird.

'We had a good time with our bird until finally we heard another kiwi calling out and the pet hearing it ran away in the night and we have never seen it again, but we still hear it cry up in the bush.'

MICHAEL, 13 years

At this time, Irene came to the school with a small bird she had found dead on the road. 'But it's not a yellow hammer is it?' she asked for she had not seen the bird so close before. She was sadly affected by this experience and wrote:

78

YELLOW HAMMER

Out by the old sheep track,
That leads into the tea-tree
The little bird lay dead
Lying with his wings under him
His eyes closed up, how sad!
The poor little bird is dead,
His legs stretched out stiffly
And his head lay lazily on to the rushes
The colours on his body shone
As the half light peered through the tea-tree.
The light sparkled on to the dead bird
That lay on the ground.

IRENE, 13 years

Pio attempted to bring his pet seagull to school by enticing it after the school bus, but it came only a little way. Some of us saw this bird and we all heard the story. Pio had taken it from its nest when it was very young but old enough to survive.

'I always test them with crumbs of bread. If they eat they are just right to take,' he said. He kept his bird at home, and gradually it grew up and he taught it to fly, so he thought. After a year it flew away, but he saw it often after that and he said it came home to feed when it seemed hungry for bread.

Clifton went on with his own affairs, wrote his story, *Last Night*, and did his lino cut and print of the *Separator Shed*.

LAST NIGHT

'Last night when I got home from school I changed my clothes and went down to watch Dad and Varley and when I got down there Varley put me on the roof and told me to tread on all the nails because I might go through and when I wanted to get down, I looked over the side of it, but then I went onto the separator roof.'

CLIFTON, 8 years

Separator shed by Clifton

79

For a time after this no topic of general interest was followed, and stories such as David's *Lewi's Letter*, Valerie's one hundred and fifth story called *Last Night* (there is cause for comment when her story is called something else), Muriel's *Sink*, Irene's *Baby Heron*, and the older Mary's *Last Night* were received. These are typical of the personal sort of writings that appear almost daily from someone.

LAST NIGHT

'Last night after I had got home from school and after I had my afternoon tea, I was just going for the cows when Clifton said he was going too so I said "All right, you can go by yourself and take your dog," and I ran where Ted was going up to the corner of the paddock to see if he could see any pheasants; I went with him.

'Soon we were on our way again going through the long hay, logs, branches, anything. Ted said, "Hey you fellows we will take short cuts." We didn't know this one so we said, "All right, oh but it's getting dark." We took his short cut but now I wished we hadn't. I wished we had gone the long way. He got across safely, but Cliff got halfway across, and he fell in the water, SPLASH. He got wet and I knew he would too; so I held onto the ginger leaves and some flax leaves. No sooner had I let go to fly across to the other side than SPLASH and I went in too. Anyhow I managed to get across but I had my right side wet with rusty water and my right gumboot was filled with water.

'Anyway I got home and had a good wash and put on my home clothes because it was my school dress that I had got wet. I washed it out, my petticoat and pinny too. Cliff had his school pants and shirt on, but he had his long pants on top of his school ones. Lucky he never got those dirty.'

VALERIE, 11 years

LAST NIGHT

'Last night as I lay restlessly on my bed I could hear the humming of the phone wires and the crying of the moreporks. Then suddenly everything was as quiet as anything. The only thing that I heard was the wind as it whispered in the rafters of our house, then to the hedge, just outside our lawn.

'The trees seemed to whisper to each other as the wind went past them to the hills beyond our place. But when the moon came out again the place was as ghostly as it was the night I was waiting at the same hour for my aunt to come home from the beach. The shadows of the trees were like figures moving around in the light of the moon. Then all of a sudden I was dreaming of far away places.'

MARY H., 14 years

THE SINK

'When I let the water out of the sink it moans and laughs down the plug hole. I like to keep putting my hand over it to make it go loud and soft. It sometimes seems to echo down the plug hole until it turns a corner in the pipe and then it stops. It sounds like a giggling girl or boy.

'I get a torch and look down the plug hole to see what it is doing on the way down. Sometimes it goes round and round and then goes laughing away down the hill.'

MURIEL

The sink, by Muriel

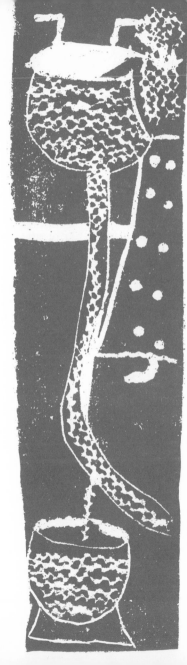

THE BABY HERON

'Last Saturday I wandered around the rocks and it was so calm that it made the shells glitter. Meanwhile seagulls fluttered above me and gannets dived under the water. Suddenly I saw in the distance a baby blue heron with his beak opening and shutting again and his eyes gleaming in the sun. And his shining soft feathers. I was thinking as I walked along.

'I saw blobs of jelly fish lying on the shore
Waves were crashing on the shore.
Sometimes drifting sticks appeared in the distance.'

IRENE

MY TEA

'Last night I had marrow and liver (but it never had any white spots in it), potato, kumara (sweet potato) and cabbage. When we began to eat, knives and forks chattered and rattled.

'Soon we began to enjoy the food we had put in front of us. When we finished plates scraped together. Soon there was something I liked. Would you have a guess? It was ice cream, boy oh boy did I eat! Soon the dishes had to be washed and as they were put in they scraped together. The knives scraped together as the water came out of the tap. Water went down to the hill like this . . . ssh sh sh sh . . . splash . . . splosh. I am the water pipe I suck water down, down, down, sssssss . . . sss sssk . . . sssssk kooo . . . swoooo swooo.'

DAVID W.

THE TEA

The tea makes you funny as can be
It is a hush tea; it goes for you
Hush a bye on the tree top,
Goodnight tea.
Makes yourself as good as gold,
The gold.
The gold is a wonderful thing;
It is a happy gold.
Gold go to sleep.
He bites all the little dogs' feet.

MARGARET

I found it imperative to foster this type of writing in preference to derivative writings. For a child can only grow in himself if he comes to grips with his environment as it affects him, and I have always felt that topical writing has always tended towards the idea of being 'occupied' with writing rather than occupied with living. Margaret's experimental thought-ramblings were written for the satisfaction of saying the words, but even this

was a way of searching out ideas. I watched her writing this small piece over a period of several minutes, then she re-read it, screwed it up and flicked it into a nearby waste-paper tin. I wondered why she should do this, so I retrieved the paper and showed her that I was interested in the poem. It was a while before others began this form of writing.

FROST

'Early this morning I saw in the frost three Maori horses standing still in the frozen frost, with their tall ears sticking straight up, and standing like dead stones on the road. In a minute or two they stamped on the curled grass and made it straight. Then the ice on the grass melted into the soil and the water went away for ever.'

BEVIN

ROCK POOL

In a little rock pool
A little starfish likes to hide
Under the rock.
In a little rock pool
He likes to hide.
Away from all enemies under the rock,
Where no one goes.
No one goes under the rock
Where the starfish hides.

CLIFTON

LEWI'S LETTER

'Dear Sir,

I have a plastered leg now but soon I'll have a walk-ing-plaster on my leg. It's much thicker on the bottom so it won't break to bits.

'There are some hard cases in this hospital, one of them is Gloria. I don't know the other one's name. There is a Scotsman here too. When he was at school he got belted and belted. One time he ran around the school and the teacher got wild and he couldn't hit him any more. That shows what Scotchmen are like.

'The wildest thing here is the injection; it's just like an arrow going into me. There's been two thermometers broken. The last one was broken on the concrete. I hope things are all right at school.

Sincerely,

LEWI.'

TWO BAD BOYS

'One Wednesday two bad boys came to Grandma's and asked her for a gallon of petrol. Grandma said that she had none in the drum and that they had to ask Jonny for some. Jonny gave them a gallon. They went down towards the outboard motor. When they arrived at the outboard they found that salt water had got into the motor. They sent me up to take the kahawai to Jonny and to get a crescent spanner, then Johnny came down. They asked him to clean the spark plug. He cleaned the spark and it went. When they got out they started and went off.

Two bad boys, by Bevin

'Mr Turvey the policeman rang grandma and asked her to ring him if she saw them. They stole a boat from Lionel Thompson and some bedding and some tinned stuff from Cable Bay. On Saturday night Wally Adams and the police arrested them.'

OWEN

CAUGHT FOR STEALING

'On Wednesday afternoon of last week I was going to my uncle's place when I caught up with two pakeha boys who were going down the beach. We watched the two boys push their boat out and try to start the motor. After a few minutes they rowed back to shore and tried to fix it. When it was fixed they rowed out and tried again, but it wouldn't start so they rowed out to sea.

'About half past seven Johnny Foster came over and asked if we had seen the two boys and we said yes we had. Then he told us that they were going to Awanui, and we said how did he know? Then he said he had been speaking to them.

'My uncle rang Mr Turvey and told him about the two boys. He however, asked my uncle if he knew where they were going and uncle said they were going to Awanui.

'Later on at about ten o'clock that night Mr Turvey rang over and said that the two boys had stolen a motor-bike from Wanganui, then they had come down to Awanui, then to Taipa, where they had stolen Lionel Thompson's boat. He said to look out for them.

'On Sunday afternoon when my uncle came back from fishing he had with him a floundering torch, a rudder from a boat, a shopping bag and there was a mattress that was still in the boat. These things he found on Norman's coast.'

WILLIAM

The children's excitement and interest in such matters as this is understandable, and it was soon to become an active part of our work each week, in that I came to expect each child to write a report on some matter of interest. Reports on visitors have always been popular, and in these I have often been astonished at the reporter's keen observation of minor habits and mannerisms. The tasks were many, such as writing invitations to school functions, regular letters to England, and always letters to any member of the school who happened to be away for a while.

Bevin found the story very exciting and he wanted to illustrate Owen's and William's account. Although the reportage tends to be less creative than the personal writings we found that work such as Bevin's lino cut helped the children towards a higher class of writing and 'illustration'. I have always looked upon this work as a discipline, for we attempted to write as clearly and concisely as possible.

6

A NEW DEPARTURE

As time went by it became increasingly clear to the children that some parts of both poetry and prose were much better than the rest. Nell's poem *Seaweed* is a case in point: of the four verses the first two were thought by everyone to make up a complete poem. Long poems (and Nell's would have been so classed at this stage) presented the seemingly insoluble problem of avoiding one or two less sincere thoughts that marred the sequence of ideas. There was a limit, too, to which the children could be taken in polishing a poem or story, before they lost interest. I remember a particular discussion on a piece of writing about walking through the mud after a flood. We tried to find the parts of the piece that were of better value, and we were getting ourselves into trouble rather than finding the solution. Then Valerie, like so many that day, felt the situation getting out of hand, so she said, 'The mud slushes under my toes but the grass likes it.' It was this cheerful thought that made us see that we could select as we saw fit, and often as not it was the small intense thing that would be taken out and away from the worse element.

SEAWEED

Under the blind seawater
The bubble fingered seaweeds
Dance and run around in airy water.

They never seem to sleep
And never seem to break the surface
Or dance too heavily.

The sun does never beat upon them
And they are never afraid of a drop of water
Because it is well and truly wet down there.

And on the darkly shaded rocks
The limpets spit and cling.

NELL

The children selected the first two verses as poems in themselves, but the third was rejected. 'This one,' Mary said, 'isn't real enough because it talks about things we don't know.'

'Maybe she was thinking about having a bath,' said someone. The children then selected the last verse as another small but separate poem.

'Limpets spitting is good,' said Irene. 'I make 'em spit sometimes, but if I knock them quickly before they cling on, I sometimes can bang them off.'

'Spit and cling is really good,' mused someone else, 'It really happens.' I began to see that the simple lyric with its single thought was more suited as a form of poetry for the children.

Before we began personal writing the children had generally written a couple of pages, out of which there might have been a line which represented real child's thinking. This sometimes appeared true for poetry. The amount presented was often no more than a quarter of a page, but that represented much more genuine thought than the previous two pages. I saw, too, that children often called a piece of writing, poetry, if it contained more than an ordinary amount of feeling.

Somehow the children misinterpreted my anxiety over the quality of the work, and wrote long poems which often did not sustain the desired feeling. I did not want length, but quality of expression. We did not think we could go on writing and accepting work that was not of the best value. When I read a piece out to the class the children could select the parts that they thought were of greater value, and they became quite skilled in their criticism of both good and bad writing.

It now seemed that poems had to be reduced in size, so that the children would be receiving the satisfactions of having created something of quality. This meant as well that they would be confirmed in the need for

Tree noises, Irene, 13 years

sincerity in thinking and writing. We examined our writings more critically and wrote small poems. At this time I introduced the children to small Japanese and Chinese poems, which gave rise to a great burst of enthusiasm for poetry writing.

The simpler poems, such as *The Pine Tree* by Irene and *Tree Noises* by Mary, *Morning* by Christopher, *Mayflies* by Valerie, *Wind* by David I., and *Thunder* by Clifton were soon largely displaced by fuller and more extensive verses, but they still followed the pattern of thought about the one idea. These came to be known by the children as 'picture poems' and from time to time in later years the same kind of poetry was written. As a poetic form it has never been entirely displaced. The children also did accompanying pictures in oils and tempera. They were not so much illustrations as alternative expressions of the ideas of the poems. The lino prints all had the same clarity and simplicity of line and content. *The Pine Tree* was illustrated with a picture of a pine tree in terms of that thought alone, and most of the 'illustrations' done at this time had the same poetic feeling. *Tree Noises* and *Wild Ducks* were two of the more successful prints for 'picture' poems at this time.

THE PINE TREE

The pine tree stands
With cracked sooted arms
With stumped branches
Rotted into the ground.

IRENE, 13 years

Wild ducks, Bevin, 13 years

87

TREE NOISES

Like the noise of wrapping papers
Comes the sound of the dead tree leaves
Blown in the wind.

MARY, 12 years

GUM TREE

The gum trees rattle like tambourines
Till the skin has come off.

MARY

THIS MORNING

This morning I could see
The dew on the grass,
Like chips of glass.

CHRISTOPHER, 11 years

MAYFLIES

Skimming over rusty red water
Skim the mayflies
The agile mayflies.

VALERIE

THE WIND

As the wind blows along
I see a little bird
Flying in the wind
So I thought I might follow it.

DAVID I., 7 years

WASHING

Slowly as I wash
The froth foams up
And is snow on a mountain.

VALERIE, 10 years

THUNDER

The thunder is the drum
When I bang it with my hands
It is the thunder.

CLIFTON, 8 years

The writing of 'picture' poems became a very popular activity and the satisfactions became very intense ones. Any poem that pleased the children was considered to be a statement of considerable merit and the result of good craft. Developments took place in many directions at this stage. Irene wrote further on her pine topic; others followed suit. Individual children wrote again and again on the same topic, and more than often the poems reflected a very intense interest in or reaction to some part of the environment.

Rosalie wrote often about the dark night, Nell about the shivery bob grass, and Lorna wrote about grass too, but without the knowledge of Nell's work. 'Picture' poems had become an established art form.

PINE TREE ON A HILL

From our house on top of the far hill
I can just see
The twin figures of the burnt pine trees
Far away like people standing.

IRENE

GRASS

Even after a year
We can still see crawler marks
In the grass
That makes drains
That flow from the hills

BERNARD

FERNS

Lying in the fern is a log
Rotting
And people sit on it
And a centipede
Lies under it.

CLIFTON

GIRLS

Girls running around
In the wind
Skirts rise
Like turkeys' tails.

BARBARA, 10 years

EVENING

Evening has come at last
Sheep away up on the hill
Like lumps of stone:
Crinkled shadows
In the paddock.

ROSALIE

SHIVERY BOB GRASS

The shivery bob blows lonelily
On its thin dusty stalks
By the road,
When the dust clouds fly over the road.

NELL

SHIVERY BOB

As the wind gently blows
The shivery bob nods and dances
The tinselly nobs are like fans
They spread by the hundreds.

NELL

SHIVERY GRASS

Shivering, shivering
In the wind.
Shivering without any wind.
Shiver, shiver,
Like me in the cold.
The wind stops
It still shivers.

LORNA

PEACHES

The peaches which belong to our river orchard are ripe
But the ones that grow beside our house on top of the hill
Are green and raw.

BARBARA

IN THE MORNING

This morning was still
And I could hear an outboard motor
On someone's boat
And away over the hills I could hear
The roaring and shouting of Waimahana's waves.

TED, 11 years

WAIMAHANA

Down Waimahana's old tracks
I go to the beach,
I see the bones of the dead cows
Lying in the grass, under the logs,
Sticking out like branches
In between the grass.

LEWI, 11 years

DISCED PADDOCKS

Crickets crying under rotting boards
While the ploughed land that overlaps
One another
Lies stiffly on the hillside and is quiet.

BARBARA

Tree design by Eric

THE CLOUDS

As the sun creeps over the sky
It goes behind the clouds
But comes out again
When the crickets chirp.

CLIFTON

SHELLS

In the shingle chattering shells
Crackle in heaps
Their pretty colours showing.

ANNA

COWS

Away down in the man high fern
Cows are roaming
With shiny backs showing.

OWEN

CRABS

As the two-way crabs scuttle
Along the rocks,
The sea gulls cry out loudly
'Come out, come out.'

VALERIE

MOREPORK

There's a morepork in that tree
Yes, in that pine tree.
If I could get my hands on him
He'd have raw meat
And nice mice tremendously fat.

VALERIE

FISH

Lying on the beach
Out on the sand by the sea
Are the bones of dead fish
Washed into the burning sand.

ROSY

DEAD BIRD

The dead bird that lies weakly
On the hot sand
Is buried by the swift blowing wind;
A few feathers sticking out of the sand.

DAVID H.

FISH

The silver bellied fish
Flick, flick from the worm baited line
In the drain.
But slowly from the dark weeds
Rises a fierce looking eel.

TED

DEAD PINE TREE

Standing lazily over the hills
Are dead pine trees
The finger-tipped spirits.

BARBARA

BLACKENED PINES

Standing in the scrubby way
Is the blackened pine
With charcoaly arms
That sway stiffly
But weakly.

VALERIE

BABY BIRDS

Baby birds open their beaks
Like open buckets;
The buckets waiting for water
And the baby birds for worms.

DAVID H.

DEAD GUM LEAVES

Lying scattered about
By dead winds
Are the 'chishing' noises
Of dry gum leaves.

IRENE

AUTUMN

Suddenly I think
Like a flash of lightning:
Summer has vanished into autumn
And all the leaves have begun to fall.

OWEN

THE WANDERING SEA

I sit on the top of the cliff and look
To the wandering sea below me
The waves slowly come up
Pushing the tangling seaweeds up with them.

MARTHA

Reeds, anon.

NOISES

As I sit in the feet-shuffling classroom
I hear the cicadas singing
But as I lie in bed at night
I hear the crawling crickets crying.

BRETT I.

AUTUMN

If autumn was here
The leaves on the trees would fall
And if John saw them
He would go and hide under them.

DAVID H.

WATTLE

The wind shorn wattles
Sway wildly today
While the blue gums rattle
Like paper in the cinders.

TED

DOWN HIHI

Where hundreds of flies
Settle on the poor cows
That are itching,
Stamping on the ground.

MAVIS

The way in which the children examined their subject of study over and over again showed me once more that there was value in concentrated study of material from their own surroundings. It had not occurred to me previously that a child could be interested in going on and on to more intensely satisfactory statements. Whenever I tried to organize the children into writing about topics in which they were not familiar the results

92

were bad. For example when they tried to write about snakes they reproduced only insincere nonsense. This convinced me that the line we were trying to develop was the right one.

Our practice was to have all the work read out in groups, preferably by the author. We then selected those papers that we liked and set them aside for a class reading and perhaps a discussion. The best work was usually published in the month's magazine. On some days nearly all the work done and read out would be acceptable for publication, but on others only one or two pieces would appeal to anybody. I think that the children may at such time have been 'saturated' with 'satisfaction' from previous successes, and have attempted to keep the feeling alive in an artificial way. I have sought other reasons for this failure, but have never found any better suggestion.

Some times poems and stories were written on the same topic by the same child. Such a case is Mary's *Telephone Wires.*

TELEPHONE WIRES

'As I sit in bed I can hear the wind blowing through the telephone wires and it is just like a mouth organ. When the wind fades away it is just like a far away sound coming from the harbour.

'When I looked at my light it blinks like my eyes and I know the kerosene light is nearly empty, but still I can listen to the far away sounds crying out because when the wind blows the wires hit apart and they ring making nice tunes.

'The sound fades away till it makes me go to sleep. I wake up at night and the harder the wind blows, the harder I can hear the telephone wires. I sat up in bed until the noises faded away.'

MARY

TELEPHONE WIRES
In the far away distance
I can hear the telephone wires
Singing in churches
Like pakehas.

After the experience of short poem writing, larger poems were again written, but were generally much better, being written with sincerity and conviction and free from the sort of second-hand thoughts that had previously spoiled the longer poems. The simple or 'picture' poetry appeared only at moments when an intense thought had been communicated or when short poems were prescribed in a writing period. At this stage I saw for the first time that very distinct individual styles had begun to show up in the work of the older children. The following poems were written because the children concerned wanted to write them. They are longer than the 'picture' poems and indicate how the children could extend their thinking and still be sincere. At this time I did not fully appreciate the value of the principle involved in this growth of the ability to express, but some years later, when there was a need to return to simple beginnings, the simple statement was again used as a beginning of poetry writing. When fifteen new children arrived in the school, I saw that they should begin from this point and not at the stage we were developing at the time.

THE DUCKS

The ducks are floating on the quiet stream
Floating along like pine needles
On the water
But the ducks which Ian shot
Are lying on the kitchen bench
All stiff.
A dead duck floating along the river
Like a pine seed
Quietly and sadly floating.

BARBARA

THIS MORNING

This morning when I awoke
Never was the sun peeping from his home
Never was a bird to be seen
And the only noise that I heard
Was a far away
Sound of sheep baaing.

DAVID H.

BIRDS

As the dozens of blackbirds fly high
in the sky
they depart like sheep down the rocks
then they go over the hills
like little dots
of sheep,
but sheep are white.

ALLAN

THE RIVER

Down by the bubbling water
Where the kingfisher dives,
From a hole in the mud ground
Around the muddy pool,
There are rank trees hanging
And beyond the pool there walks
A pukeko,
Wading in the swamp.
Away in the distance the gulls
Can hear the words of the storm approaching
So they all fly inland
And the storm comes and goes
And piles the polished driftwood and shells
Hollow as trumpets
Upon the beach—
The sandy beach.

SARAH

PAPER ON THE WALL

When the wind comes impatiently
Through the windows
It pushes the flies against the walls
And they bang annoyingly around.
It blows the paper
And makes it rustle and talk.

NELL

CRUSHED SHELLS

As I walk around the beaches
I step on to the slippery arms of the washed up
    sea-weeds,
Crushed shells lying underneath the seaweed
Hurt my feet,
The crushed shells slice into the sand
As I tread on them.

IRENE

In length and interest the stories written at this time were much like David W.'s *So Early in the Morning* and *The Thrush and Another Bird,* but David's work had become very characteristically his own. He was a boy who had been largely unaffected by the poetry development that had been going on, and in his time at this school he rarely wrote what he called a poem at all. We recognized the poetic feeling of his prose in such stories as the following.

SO EARLY IN THE MORNING

'So early in the morning when all the frost is out I go to fetch a horse and on the way I see funny pigs' tails; some are curled and some are straight. Along comes Shorty our dog, he thinks the pigs are the same as him. One pig bit him and Shorty wasn't very pleased about this so he bit the pig and ran away.

'I said to myself I can't be bothered with looking at him, the dog and the pig, so I went to catch my horse. I was thinking how nice it is to be outside in the cool.'

DAVID W.

THE THRUSH AND ANOTHER BIRD

'As the thrush sings up in the tall trees with the thin branches with his feet hanging on tightly he sings his song: ting, tong, ting and then he stops.

'He listens to another thrush sing for a while.'

DAVID W.

In all this work the production of poems or pictures or the gaining of specific facts or techniques was always secondary to the growth of the children. The Davids (there were four of them at that time) and the others developed sometimes with and sometimes without a close analysis of what they were doing. Analysis often followed after a particular trend had been noticed in their development. For example, in 'picture' poem writing, during some of the analytical sessions the children's attention was drawn to the Japanese and Chinese verse of the same nature. Similarly, in the development of the technique of 'thought' writing, which follows, they came to know and to appreciate contemporary styles in the same vein. I began to wonder a little about the effect of this when poems such as Valerie's *Hopscotch,* which is so much like Belloc's *Miranda,* started to appear.

Still, Valerie had absorbed the feeling of rhythm from that poem and made something new of it, so we accepted it.

HOPSCOTCH

Thump, thump
The stamping of feet
can be heard of the flop-footed people.
And the clack, slap of the flattened tin
Thrown,
And the hooray of the people as the player gets out
And the weary sigh lifts the air
As the player walks away
From the hopscotch patch.

VALERIE

These developments of child expression (e.g. 'picture' poetry writing) and the analysis by all of us, with 'exercises' when needed, are a necessary part of creative education. David W. was a boy who remained apart from the main stream of development but who made contact through his feeling for the work in art and crafts. He came to write just as well as most because of this. He found it hard to understand these discussions of developments, but after hearing the writing read out aloud, he seemed to absorb the feeling for it without the benefit of the 'exercises' and the analysis. The influence of children upon one another in many subtle ways was made clear to me later when newcomers to the school picked up our attitude and values quite naturally without having to go through the longer processes of development that we had followed by trial and error.

We found that certain happenings such as changes in the weather, unusual natural things or new people caught the attention of the children strongly and became the material of much writing both prose and poetry. One such a set of writings took place after an afternoon when the sky clouded over, heavy rain clouds darkened the sky, and towards evening a high wind came up. A wild storm blew and lasted all night, and so loud was the wind, the rain, and the thunder that many people woke from their sleep. Among them were Roderick and Valerie. The next day at school was hot, steamy and unpleasant. These three pieces of writing came from this experience.

LAST NIGHT

With a flicker, flicker of lightning
And crashing booming sounds of thunder
Ricochet over the sky,
Then the flicker, flicker of light
And dimness comes.
What happened?
The power went off

Two trees and man, Colin, 11 years

And the only light is the fire.
Another flicker, flicker of lightning comes
Then the ricocheting masses of thunder
Go rolling across the sky
With a crack, crack, a branch breaks in the roaring
wind.

RODERICK

THOUGHTS IN MY MIND

'The day was hot and the clouds swept over the sky;
they rushed past the sun, but the sun could never be lost;
the brightness shone through the clouds as if it didn't see
the ground and that day was as hot as fire, just like
flames drifting up into the air.

'It started when the trees shaded the ground, a caterpillar crawled forward on tiny steps and his many legs
were like furry stalks hidden deeply beneath his body;
those many legs were like sticks hanging to a branch.'

SARAH

LAST NIGHT

Last night the wind howled around the corners.
The shivering dogs huddled up into the corners of
their houses.
The quacking ducks snuggled together.

The cows hid in the tall trees, but the people in
their beds did not hear
The moans of their dogs or any of the sad cries
of the creatures outside.
Slowly but wearily the night wore on; the lost sheep
shivered
Under the dirty sky; some animals moped about till
the bleak winds died down.
The morning sun rose waking the birds; the cattle
began to graze again
And the air was filled with happiness; the bright
sun shone
Down on the cheerful earth.

VALERIE

The freedom ·of the school allowed for exceptional
expressions such as these to be recorded, but whereas
I had often thought in my own way that a certain
happening would offer the same sort of stimulation, my
expectation was rarely realized. Nor was I able to evoke
similar feelings in children that would cause them to
write in a similar way. These three had written these
pieces for themselves and they were motivated by the
real experience.

7

THOUGHT WRITING

ARAH'S story, *Thoughts in my Mind,* reminded me of Margaret's *Tea* ramblings of some time ago, which has the same underlying idea, and when the three pieces of work on the storm were discussed in the usual poetry writing and reading time, Sarah's story was particularly liked because of the *thoughts* it contained. This story was unlike the usual writing in that there is a certain amount of added feeling of freedom about content. The thoughts, apart from being rather rambling, are somewhat better and more inspiring ones. We looked at Sarah's story and enjoyed such sentences as, 'It started when the trees shaded the ground', and 'A caterpillar crawled on tiny steps.' We recalled the simplicity of the 'picture' poems, because no doubt we were thinking of the same sort of poetic beauty.

Then I asked the children to list twelve things they were thinking about and to write about them in the same way; but of course the exercise was useless, because I was asking the children to copy a style of writing and had not explained the principle to them. I saw then that if I asked the children to write, at considerable speed, all the thoughts that came into their minds without bothering about punctuation or spelling a great deal of raw material would come out which could be the basis of further work. I thought that certain subjects could reasonably be chosen by me, for any reaction would be a useful one. So I asked the children to write all their thoughts, no matter what they were, as they came into their minds. They would have to write very quickly or they would find that they could not get them down before others appeared.

I asked them to write for ten minutes without stopping, until their 'pencils were so tired' they could not write any more. I suggested that the children begin by focusing their attention within the classroom. This was not to say where their thinking would lead them.

Ten minutes of continuous concentration and recording is not an easy task, though most children managed to accomplish it. The demands of this writing are intense, perhaps more so than any other language 'activity' and the absorption is comparable with that which I have observed in the visual arts, especially when a child is planning a design. The papers were certainly untidy, the spelling was better than I expected, but I wasn't very interested in that aspect as long as I could read the copies out to the children for their comments. We were surprised at the variety of thought. I asked the children to start reading silently, in the usual way, for ideas, phrases, and clauses that appealed to them. The children produced these examples: 'I can hear the catching of the pencils and the scratching of books.' 'I can hear the squeekers in the trees.'

BRUCE, 8 years

BLOWFLIES AROUND THE CLASSROOM

Around the classroom window, the buzzing of the
   blowflies
Up and down on the windows.
Munch, munch of the cows eating roses.
Round and round the light, a creeping spider on
   the light.
Meat in the oven singeing up;
Blowflies on the elements
Walking around.
Blowflies on the light watching us.
The flickering of the light makes the flies buzz off.
Off the light goes;
In and out the crack,
Bees buzzing over the still roof.

GLENNIS, 8 years

PENCILS

Pencils, scribbling scribbling
On a blind sheet of paper.
Clock ticking
Ticking in the front of the room
Clock strike twelve, the bell echoes in the far
   distance
Noises of mouths whispering to each other.

CHRISTOPHER, 12 years

Walter liked this one about a shark mobile: 'The shark mobile is dancing before the whaler Ken made.' Allan selected this: 'Owen's noisy shoes, teeth-edging across the pine-boards.' And Walter found another about mobiles: 'Look, he dives like a bird in transparent water.'

Most of these pieces selected by the children are direct, vivid, economical, and evocative. They bring the image or the remembered feeling immediately to the reader's consciousness, so that he feels or is aware of the writer's subject quite intensely. Quality in children's writings seems to be marked by freshness, immediacy, and intensity. It is an expression of unashamed awareness, and its function is to promote more intense awareness in children of their own thoughts and feelings about the world around them. This is the direction of educational growth, towards better and more abundant life.

'I think of mice in the walls and rats in cats' teeth and unbaited traps.'

'A branch scratches bare fingers on the roofing iron.'

'Martha's looking at her brother with her pencil pointing at ten o'clock.'

'The light's brighter than I thought.'

'Pencil rivers on the desk top.'

'Ink spots my father made.'

'And I sweep the floor and the dust goes into the cracks between the boards till I sweep the floor again.'

Thus began a burst of activity in 'thought writing'. Children chose their own subjects and wrote as Martha, Rosy and Nell did.

THOUGHTS ABOUT THE TELEPHONE

I wonder if that ring is Barbara's?

What is that outside?

Someone is stamping, Christopher is looking at himself in the mirror.

He thinks he is good looking.

Our pet bird is singing out to us; the fire is out;

Oh, Bernard talks too much.

MARTHA

THOUGHTS

'As I go into my room the window is opened and I hear away in the distance a lonely morepork and for a while he keeps quiet and then he sounds his trumpet again. Suddenly sounds go away a little and I hear the river rushing down; trees swaying against each other. Then I hear the morepork again; he must have gone to a different tree, his noise sounds different.'

ROSY

THE ROAD

'Tonight as I walked along the road, I saw a smooth place on the side of the road and on it were lots of marks. Some of them were horse marks and one unusual print was a shoe mark. It had lots of marks on the heel of it and round the toe were holes as big as threepences.

'Out in the middle of the road were all different shaped stones and between them were wheel marks. I caught a glimpse of something on the ground, so I stopped to see what it was; it was a locust—"The poor thing", I said to myself. Then I said, "anyway that is one less to jump out at me and frighten me." '

NELL

What we have called *thought writing* and others have called *associative writing* seems to fit naturally many children's ways of thinking. It is the expression of their stream of consciousness, but it enhances these by making the children more aware of their own observations and thoughts.

From these beginnings Irene, a Maori girl, developed her own particular way of writing, which we recognised as relatively mature and individualistic.

Just before she left school at the age of fifteen she wrote *Thoughts, Sea Thoughts, Down the Swamp, Noises, Ponga Tree, Water on the Branches* and *Thoughts on Light*. Irene was the first child to leave the school after these developments had occurred. She had made them all part of herself and was writing work that we thought was of unmistakably poetic value.

THOUGHTS

The rain drizzles down slowly
Then for a while it goes away
Drifting far, far away.
Suddenly I hear the winter's bird
Crying out from the tree branch
Swish, swish, slush the water streams
Run roughly.
The willows bend their bodies down low,
Bowing down into the water
The poplars out on the farms
Spill their dried leaves.

IRENE, 15 years

SEA THOUGHTS

While I walked around the rocks
I heard the crabs tap, tapping in the rocks.
The seaweeds danced with even rhythms
Their arms went out in all directions.
The waves hit against the rocks
The water ran off the shelves and ledges
I heard the fighting of the seagulls
I heard the thundering wings of shags.
I watched them fly out into the rough open seas.
I walked on further listening to seasquirts that hissed
    in the hollows of the rocks
I stepped on to the beach and felt the cold sand.

IRENE

DOWN THE SWAMP

'While sitting on the bare banks where the grasses have dried and where the water has sunk into the ground in cracks, I heard a far away sound—a river sound; soon I smelt paint, but no it's mud. Then I shifted to another place under the shade of the blue gum. Suddenly my eyes caught a moving shadow stretching on the ground. The crickets began scuttling in amongst the fern and I thought for a while and a butterfly came flying by and I thought he had taken my thoughts away; now I have nothing to think of; the cicadas, the noisy ones, they tried to make me sing. Soon the butterflies came past with tent shaped wings. When they fly their wings spread out and when they land, their wings stand up like triangles, the blue triangles.'

IRENE

NOISES

The noise of dipping oars.
Night time.
Cliffs into water—
Hardly.
Rowlocks rattling as someone rows
Towards the shore;
An outboard motor in the harbour
Sometimes it fades away—
Slowly.

IRENE

rge pot decoration, David and Allan

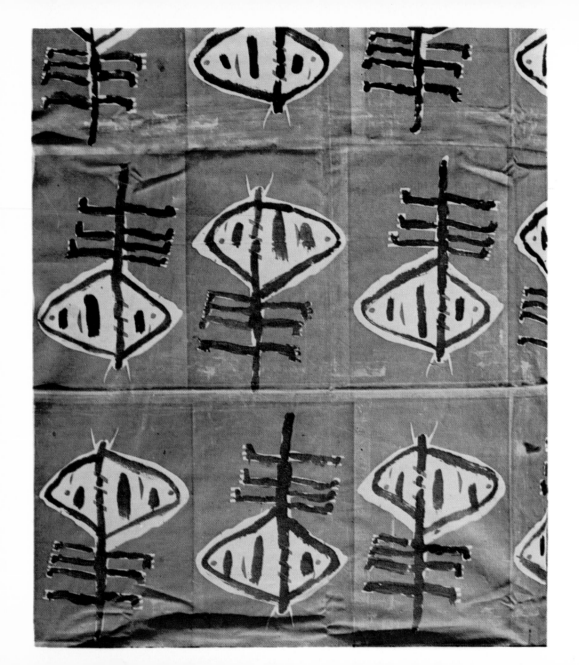

Butterfly design, Sonny

PONGA TREE

'The ponga tree has at last his new leaves. Green leaves all coming out, young ones all curled under. Smaller and smaller, many leaves, at the ends of the branches; ends. But at the side of the ponga tree there hangs dead fern leaves. Brown and old looking—sad.'

IRENE

WATER ON THE BRANCHES

'Out in our orchard I see water blobs racing along the tree branches. I watch them as they go plop onto the ground. All their leaves have come off. They have no rain coats to shelter them. The glassy water blobs hang onto the branches still.

'Suddenly a small wind came up and started to shake and move the branches. Some of the blobs skipped off the branches. For a while a shower came. All I could see of the far hills was a patch of rain still coming. Soon the shower bounced upon the roof. More blobs were on the tree again.'

IRENE

THOUGHTS ON LIGHT

English light
As Mum fills up our seven year old light
It mumbles as the kerosene rises up.
Light:
Sprinkled through the coloured curtains,
Light flits through and out the window blinds
And through it making a coloured film.
Moonlight:
Passing through the tangled bushes:
Streams:
Wading in water,
Lifting their umbrellas up to shade.
Cars:
Rustling through the tar-sealed streets;
cars and trucks passing like lightning
Waves thrashing upon a beach.
Foam bubbling below it.
Birds hiding in their nests;
Seaweed waving like cotton thread.

IRENE

'English light' needs explaining. The only form of lighting apart from candles in Irene's home was the kerosene mantle lamp, which was marked *Made in England*. In the evenings the children watched this lamp burning and it was thus an important part of their attention and hence their thinking.

I had not known that the poetry workship activities were doing anything other than give the children opportunities to become more proficient in writing. From my point of view I was most interested in assisting the children to work out the developments mentioned. I had not expected recognizable styles to develop, and indeed this only happened gradually and with the more mature children.

When the children were judging one another's work they always referred to simple images in specific phrases, and never referred to the pieces as a whole. I attempted to encourage a consideration of the whole 'architecture' of a piece now and then, but saw that only a few of the more mature children could do this.

I was constantly looking both for ways of expression characteristic of childhood, and, inside that, for characteristics of particular children, hoping to help each develop his own way of seeing, thinking about things, and expressing himself in writing. I felt that a child like Olive, who wrote *Mice* when she was five years old, should develop a style of her own and become aware of it, perhaps should even use it consciously by the time she was as old as Jenny who wrote the second poem.

MICE

Creeping mice in the garden
And our cat comes
And bounces on a mice.

OLIVE

MICE

Peeping and sneaking mice
Staring eyes,
Silently on tip toes,
And scratching claws
Cling to the bare walls
Their stealing eyes glance
Screeching around.

They pull their wire claws,
Noisy things dash out of sight
Under the lino, making no bumps—they are deadly hidden.

JENNY, 12 years

By the time they were ready to leave us Valerie, Mary, Sarah, and Ronny seemed to me to have developed quite distinct styles.

MIDNIGHT

What beautiful things that cry in the night
All the things that I can hear
Are in the shade of the kauri tree.
Stars, stars,
Bleating, fleating.
In the shadow of the night.
In the night there is the cry of the morepork
In the big kauri tree.
That has holes up there in his branches
Dark, dark,
Peck, peck.
You will never get anything,
Because it is a dark night,
When the dogs bark at you in the night.

MARY

'Fleating' in this poem was the child's own word. Quite often children made up such a word as this for the continuation of the rhythmic feeling, in this case of the bleating idea.

THE WATER

Plonk!
A stone hit another stone
Under the water.
Above the water and polished stones
A crooning seagull flies,
And with a bark and a splash
A dog chases.

VALERIE

THE HERON

I hide behind the mud hill
And oh, what do I see?
A lump of frost?
What is it?
IT'S A STRONG WHITE HERON TALL
But look it's standing on one leg stick
I see another further over the mud flat
What, what do you think?
What do I see?
Other Herons!
All peppered along the beach.

VALERIE

STEALING

How horrible and creeping like cats
People creeping and sneaking.
Devils must have tempted them
Or they were thieves before.
How wonderful, they think.

They act.
And while the people sleep,
Unknown and unseen by others,
Thieves creep up to the shops
And without looking back,
Their enemies who are their foot steps,
Follow them through the dust floors.

SARAH

ROLLING HILLS

Away out in the distance,
And over the far, far hills
The thunder sat speaking
To the talking tree leaves.
As they mumbled in the wild wind
Many moaning sounds
Showed their tall lumpy bodies
And spoke more like the thunder.
Again the voice of the growling thunder
Spoke
And bounced and seemed to push the hills down
For he spoke so loudly and so angrily.

SARAH

THE RAIN GAUGE HORSES

Around and around and backwards and forwards,
The scampering-fit horses gallop and buck,
'It's going to rain,' I said
'Horses make good rain gauges.'

Whenever it rains their drumming feet can be heard
    all over the paddocks.
Their screaming calls ring out all over the farms,
Bang, bang, bang, thumpety, thump.
The drum sound feet pattern the paddocks.

RONNY

HERONS

In the wet depths of the sloshy mudflat
Two tall and long legged birds stride
Slowly and steadily
Up the crab-holed edges
Looking for food.
Slap, slap as their rooster like feet
Hit the sloshy and slimy mud,
And every now and again they tip their tails
and lean over their long legs
And ram their stalky beaks
Into the mud for something to eat.

RONNY

I have noted that several things took place as these children progressed and as they were confronted by a programme in which plain factual knowledge on aspects of literature are given, such as accent. Essay work is all too often unrelated to the child's real experience and as well the natural flow of children speech rhythms are denied their expression if types of sentences are taught. Again the intelligent child 'excels' through his absorption of the facts of this artificial approach. Poetry, such as is written, is within established forms of the early part of the century and earlier. It has set rime and rhythm, and follows patterns which again deny the child the opportunity to use his natural flow of language. The verse is thus poor and insincere and in no way can be compared to the personal expression of previous years. In one or two instances I noted that 'success' in some examination through competence in these higher school methods and materials was enough to make the children concerned feel that creative methods are not related to the realities of examinations, the synonym of success. On the other hand there are many who saw that their secondary education was concerned with poorer values and they held on to their established standards throughout and after this experience.

Beetle fabric design by Eliza

8

LANGUAGE TECHNIQUES

FOLLOWING the first work with thought writing about things in the classroom and our attempts to select the valuable elements from a mass of thought, I tried to direct the children's attention to other subjects, at first a series of familiar places.

If I asked the children for an ordered essay on one of the many *places* they knew, they would generally fail, as the process of essay writing on a given topic so proves. Thought writing about a place does not need to be concerned with a story. The child's knowledge of a washhouse, for example, is based on a number of observations of various different aspects of such a room, and I am inclined to think that children become interested in one aspect at a time—the copper fire, the soot, or the wood heap. He will examine the copper again and again; then perhaps he will experiment with the fire and feed it. I have had much evidence from the children's writings that supports the idea that they establish a familiarity with a place on the basis of numerous unrelated aspects of it. They may know a lot about daddy-longlegs, spiders, the copper fire, wetas in the firewood, the smell of soap, and the stain of the 'blue' in the wooden tubs long before they establish relationships between these things. Thought writing about such a place seems, indeed, to aid their seeing of such relationships. In many ways this understanding by the child of intimate details about the spiders, the fire, the stream, and the dark corners as a continuous set of things that relate each to each, explains why children cannot write essays that adequately tell *all* about a washhouse and wash-day even if they call their minds to the task. Nor can they make criticism of a piece of such writing as a whole. I pointed out earlier what the child does to the detailed imagery and what he recognises as characteristic of himself and his thinking. As he writes his thought he records these associated ideas as a stream of conscious recollections. If and when the child does this, and if he does it often enough, I believe he becomes able to make larger and larger criticisms of literature at his own level and, in time, of the writings of other people. This sort of experience allows children to develop their powers of reasoning in terms of literary criticism.

Although the rather blunt approach of the direct

request for ten minutes' thought writing to a set topic such as the kitchen proved reasonably successful, we found that a great number of places about the school and home could be introduced into writing through painting, writing, and drama. In each situation I saw that the children were able, through being freed from a demand for exactness in writing, to come nearer to describing their real experiences and their inner thoughts. It seemed reasonable to ask for a stream of thoughts starting from any subject I chose, for the mind saw that the individual was not damaged or diminished as he might be if he has to write at length about a subject that he knows little about.

May's *Warmth of the Kitchen,* Rudolf's *I Went to the Apple Tree,* Clifton's *Fireback* and Glennis's *Hills* indicate the kind of writing that comes from this type of request.

WARMTH OF THE KITCHEN

'The warmth of the kitchen; the stove with the red hot elements smoulders with heat. The cupboard door swinging backwards and forwards. The dribble of the sink tap dripping to the sink; the egg beater buzzing.'

MAY, 13 years

I WENT TO THE APPLE TREE

'I went to the apple tree, I was talking. My father said, "Be quiet." Mum hit the dog with the broom. I kicked another dog. Eric said, "Come out of the rain." '

RUDOLF, 8 years

FIREBACK

The sooty curved fireback
Where the goats stand and flicker
And go out.
And the flames rush up and knock them off
And they go up the chimney.

CLIFTON

HILLS

Scrub hills, sheep tongued hills, sheep tramped hills,
Mountain hills, rabbiter hills.
The brown patches blind my eyes;
Scrub pointed out like rows of trains that drive
    along the rails
Sheep happy, quietly eating.
Starlings picking the ticks off the patchy green hills
Twitchy heads move up above the bluegum trees.
Sheep rub on the bark trunks, dead gorse, live gorse
Growing on the hills.

GLENNIS

In some cases the children were taken to visit various places and the same sort of work was repeated. This certainly aided the flow of thoughts and helped the smaller children to become aware of their environment.

Olive's piece is not so matter-of-fact as her previous *Mice,* written a year earlier, and shows how quickly a young child may become conscious of style, while Fenella's piece is an outstanding statement for an otherwise not very expressive person. 'I hear the idgiebidgies (the native cicada) go crick, crick, crick', and her observations of the blowfly chasing the piece of paper are the kind of observations we liked.

A PLACE

'When we went for a walk I heard the long-tongued dogs barking; buzzing bees busy in nests. Short-beaked birds were singing sweetly in cool-leafed trees, which reflected in the cool twisted river. I heard the leaves rustling softly and light-winged cicadas singing. I saw the long shadows of trees dancing in the water. The flax flowers hung heavily on broken stems.

'I could hear birds singing, popping buds, shivering trees, rippling waters, romping leaves.

'I could see bubbles rising, a tree a-swinging, buzzing bees, smooth stones and little chirping birds.'

OLIVE, 6 years

A PLACE

'A bit of paper blown down the path and a nosy fly chases it.

'I see shadows dancing in the river; throwing sticks in the river. Sticks make rings, they grow bigger and bigger and make one big lovely one.

FENELLA

From this approach, a series of possible tasks was drawn up in a list from which the children chose their own excursions to the outside.

1. *Go and find several very beautiful stones.*

2. *Go and look at the bikes in the shed.*

3. *Watch the drains working. Turn on a tap.*

4. *Go and look at the corner post* (where there was a starling's nest).

This direction led to David's *Blackbirds* (a small perceptual error, but a good story—he meant Starlings).

BLACKBIRDS

'Blackbirds that sing all day up in our rough spacy pine tree, where the branches sprout out in all designed ways and where the sparrows live in thousands.

'Blackbirds that fight for nests away up in our chimneys and under the roofs of our houses and in the strainer posts in the corner of our garden where our cat, Tom, tries, tries to catch him.

'My blackbird is too cunning for Tom. But Tom, our cat, has five sons growing (and they have long tails) and they are getting as big as their father. Days are going quickly.

' "No," says the cat Tom, "We must keep trying to catch that blackbird; his babies will be flying soon; his babies are growing fast, and they are nice and fat." Just then the blackbird flew out and by the time Tom got there, Tom said, "The blackbird has a nice nest." (the bird had gone). "He has a smooth hole and when he goes down, he just slides down. You and I are just young now, but our sons will help to catch some birds when they grow older." '

5. *Go for a walk to the ploughing next door.*

This led to Clifton's *Seagulls*.

6. *Look down a crack in the concrete.*

7. *Listen to the sounds of the swamp.*

Extensive poetry and stories such as Sarah's arose from this observation.

SEAGULLS

'The seagulls flew in mobs across our paddock and some flew away and landed on the hill next to ours and then one by one they glided down and turned a circle and landed in our paddock by the drain which leads down to our pigsty and another one flew down and landed with the rest of the seagulls. Then our dog, Wally, chased them and they flew and turned a circle again and landed by the drain in the same place. They cooed at each other as they were pecking and scratching for worms.'

CLIFTON

SOUNDS OF THE SWAMP
Closed the doors of sound
Near the sucking swamp,
Wandered by bitterns.
Bubble, bubble,
Up rise the sounds.

Ears of the swamp
Damp and clear,
Cleaned the birds
From a distance
Quietened the noises

Boiling around the edges
Like wild squawkers.
Swiftly shivering in ease are birds,
Airing their soft feathers in sound.
JENNIFER, 12 years

Jennifer first heard the silence in the swamp, but soon she became aware of new kinds of noise, such as the 'bubble, bubble' of swamp gases. Her attention is taken with the ideas of various kinds of sounds and hearing throughout. When she wrote 'ears' she was overlapping the two ideas of 'airs' and 'ears'. That she intended both meanings, without having the technical knowledge of an adult poet, makes the poem all the more remarkable. The idea that sound is a tangible quantity as well as the 'air', and the air although damp is also 'clear', implying sound, is outstanding. She explains the movements of

110

birds drying wings, 'cleaned the birds' in as compact a use of words as any poet could achieve. There is an imaginative feeling about 'boiling around the edges, like wild squawkers' which isn't explained fully.

As a child she did not have the experience to deal with the technical problems (they, however, would have puzzled most adult poets) but the ideas and images make this a marvellous poem.

SWAMP

'As I push my way past the swamp, I looked around and saw the rusted water stained in my dog's fur. Gently I pushed my way past, closing my eyes so that the wiwi* wouldn't find their way quite so easily in. Now it is altogether too late for I had fallen into the sloshy swamp water hole. Struggling to get out, I could see my dog in the same way, struggling with all his might.'

SARAH

8. *Listen to the Telephone Posts.*

'I press my ear to the humming telephone pole; it sounds like the sea far, far away. I think of the traffic in the city. I see something close to my eyes. I take my ear away and kill an ant. I slowly put my ear back and the noises come closer, like a wave it comes loud all of a sudden as I put my ear close. I tramp on a stick that snaps and then I run and walk back out of the telephone

Wiwi is a Maori word for rushes.

hum. I think I can still hear it when I'm across the road. I look back at the long pole across the road that a long crack has run down. I walk back and look into it and press my ear close to it and think of what I might write.'

9. *Feel the shape of a tree or branch.*

FEELING A PINE CONE IN MY HAND

'The textured pine cone round and pointed like a dotted shoe, chapping in the palm of my hand with unusual feeling and pressing shell designs on the linings of the palm of my hand. Slipping from my fingers. Curiously landing in the twigs. Spare gaps shaded the dark colours of the rough cone. Slowly pushing the stalks of grass, leaving shadows of a sharp figure behind, hidden in the shape of the moss, covered with hints of soil.'

JENNIFER

10. We found it useful to write about unfamiliar things that were still close enough to our experience to warrant some attention. Some of these were imaginative ideas such as that of the inside of a bottle, the inside of the red hot kiln, inside an engine. Then there were topics such as the engine of a car which Mavis wrote about.

ENGINES

'The noise is all that I can understand. Noise is all that I know and understand.'

MAVIS

I helped the children to look further into their study of places and to see every detail and details within details, and to think also, of their own changing feelings about the places and about their looking; people can be just as interesting as places, especially the self. Personal feelings such as instances of love, hate, and fear, are also useful beginnings. Thoughts about story or historical happening can also be fun for children.

The experience of going to observe some phenomenon such as the starling in the corner post did not imply that the child should write about that happening, but often as not they did. Whereas most of this sort of writing was fit to present to other children, there remained much that was really a collection of what appeared to be haphazard wanderings. But it appeared that thought wanderings could all be about one topic such as Glennis's Shop, in which points of experience are lighted by a thought here and there. The whole is quite acceptable as prose or poetry, whatever the child desires to call it. Glennis called this one, *Shop*.

There are bananas that I can see;
there are drinks on the shelves,
ice-cream in the freezer as hard as bullets,
When I see something, my mouth gets hungry.
Beer and biscuits and bottles on the shelves
Waiting for someone to take them home.
Wood for shelves. Rotten iron on the roof.
Sweets that smell, waiting for people.

Chewing gum chewing, chewing gum, glop, chop,
Their teeth crack against the chewing gum.

The recognition of small excellences had been part of our experience with criticism of poetry and prose writing so that Glennis's piece was praised for the 'elements' of expression as well as the whole 'architecture' of the piece. 'Beer and biscuits and bottles on the shelves. I like to say that,' said Mavis. 'Wood for shelves. That reminds me of the feeling I got from that poem you read us last term, Sir, by a fellow of the same name as the Australian four-minute miler.'

'Eliot wasn't it?' added Tim.

'He beat the four-minuter if I remember correctly,' someone said.

'What, at poetry or running?'

'It's still a good feeling,' said Tim.

Some *thoughts* wandered from one idea to another, as in Ken's *Happy Sounds*.

HAPPY SOUNDS

'A warm feeling is going through my body and noises wander about outside. Rattling of windows banging backwards and forwards. Pots on the ledge, their designs wriggling around them. Our paintings on the wall, they look around them. Mobile trees in the wind. Birds flying hardly, around them.'

In this piece Dennis and Ken marked several thoughts that they agreed were better than others and that might interest the rest of the writing group that morning. 'Pots on the ledge, their designs wriggling around them' and 'a warm feeling is going through me', 'mobile trees in the wind'. We recorded these separately on a page which we headed 'We Liked These Thoughts'.

We published sheets of such statements in our monthly magazine, but I felt that we should make more of these interesting thoughts. Ken's paragraph does not say much about anything, but as we saw earlier some altogether unsatisfactory writings later blossomed into stories of real value. I felt, too, that if I asked Ken to try to develop one idea on the basis of one or two associated thoughts about it we might again expect a process of some satisfaction to overtake him.

Ken took his ideas away to work on, for he quickly saw that the continuity of some writings such as Glennis's was missing in this piece. His approach was not wrong, and I did not want him to think it was. He began thinking more deeply into his subject and came back soon after with an expansion of his ideas, *Mobile Trees*.

MOBILE TREES

I can see
Out
Of the window
On the very, very very top
Of a tree
A sparrow is balancing
Himself.

Trees mobile around
And birds are flying hardly,
Their feathers stick up like roosters wild.

KENNETH

BLOWFLIES IN THE CLASSROOM

Early in the afternoon when the cows come home;
Around the rose bush, munch, munch of the cows
Eating the roses.
But in the house where the flies buzz,
The flickery of the light
Makes the flies buzz off.

GLENNIS

Ken could well write about 'the pots on the ledge, their designs wriggling around them' or the work of birds and trees. In a similar way children select one idea, shape, or design from a painting and they develop this and associated ideas into painting of greater satisfaction to all of us. This process suited some people more than others. Mary, Jennifer, and Mavis rarely had to reconsider such a piece of writing, but Glennis and Ken used this process often. We felt more justification for our inclusion of the pages of 'Thoughts We Like' in our publications.

THOUGHTS WE LIKED

I hear the thistle seeds crackling.

BRUCE, 8 years

113

The flickering light wears its dripping candle to an end.

DENNIS, 10 years

People look like flowers with clean faces.

MARILYN, 8 years

Dirty things with stalking feet.

MAURICE, 8 years

Wiwi sheep tunnels.

CLIFTON, 11 years

CENTIPEDE

I poked it and it flung its head and
twisted its crawling body and a
little centipede-feeling twig touched
my leg. I ran for my life onto the
lovely-feeling grass.

ERIC, 12 years

Shell shapes curled round and round
Like leaves long fallen
Curved and brown,
Earth coloured and dead.

ANONYMOUS

This was a piece of writing that I picked up from the floor. We couldn't recognise the hand—an argument against uniform cursive writing.

A study of spiders and flies begun about this time provided the first pages of what we came to call the full value of our work. Every thought, even the single image, that was thought of value was collected for our next publication. This gave the children an immediate feeling of intense 'belonging' to the magazine, and gave a tremendous impetus to the quantity of their imaginative statements.

The wind-trembled web with cross bars closed.

GLENNIS

Wolf spiders pounce like cats catching birds and mice.

MARILYN

I give the spider a poke and it spins its long elbowed legs. Sometimes it trembles to itself.

GLENNIS

The Daddy-long-legs shaking in the soft breeze of day wind. I poke him with my lively finger.

WALTER

Waiting for a careless spider to come and get caught in the thin thread of its soft web.

CLIFTON

Spiders climbing on web painted walls.

ERIC

Spider hunters, catching silver leg-paralysing spiders and taking them and walling them up with mud banks.

ERIC

SPIDERS

'When I poke the spinning spiders they spin dizzily around. Sometimes I pull his long elbowed legs off and I poke him a little with a burnt black stick. When I let him crawl on my hand, I squeeze him and he dies dead in my hand, curled up.'

ERIC

Spider by Eric

DADDY-LONG-LEGS

'The daddy-long-legs spins around and around and goes in and out like a cement crusher. He crawls up the roof, sticks his glue, then slides down; down like a sinker on a line. I gave him a poke and he spun around the other way, but faster. When I stopped poking him, he rocked on his web bouncing on his long spindly legs, then he slows down until he is really still. He crawls away up to the roof and can't be seen any more so I go and look for another one and do the same thing.'

JOHN M., 11 years

DADDY-LONG-LEGS

Daddy-long-legs quickly spinning around
A giant finger poked softly on its jointed body;
Then its legs folded in and out and playing exercises.
It scrambled up the rotting board, hung from its
    spinnerets
And pushed downwards, not touching
And the air bounced it upwards.
A sticky web waited unharmed . . . a long bent
    spider crept
A stiff fly homed to the glued web.

JENNIFER, 13 years

'Little flies with their fans on their sides.'

ELIZA, 12 years

'Fingers have mouths that swallow up the buzzing
    flies.'

CLIFTON

'I poked the spider and he went around like a fly in a web.'

BRUCE

'Which way did he turn? What would he do when I poke him: Would he do it or not? Would he run away if I went up to him? Was he a daddy-long-legs: Was it a male or a female? Where was its web? Did it have a web? Did it have any babies? If it did, where did it keep them? And do they know their mother?'

JOHN M.

Glennis wrote a more intense statement about spiders. This and her *Starfish* are triumphs for a girl of only average intelligence. I felt that she was successful because she reconsidered her subject before going on to write again. Reconsideration seems to be a primary principle of creative education.

FLIES SWALLOWED IN GIANT'S FINGERS

Flies that are swallowed in the big hearty giant
    fingers
That clang together under the figure's face
Tame people looking
Wild people running away.

STARFISH

In the dark limpid pools
In the blue blossom pool

On the numb-footed rocks

116

The scattered starfish whisper
On the blurred seaweed.

The brown bubbled seaweeds,
Floated on the blossom waters.

It lay on the skin-footed rocks
Lying dead, swept up
On the rocks.

GLENNIS

I was left wondering after these experiences. How was it that many preferred the simple statements of small poems to the larger and more detailed prose accounts of the same thing. I concluded that it was because the longer work did not approach the quality of, say Glennis's, that all children had in them a gift of seeing directly and a talent for expressing their vision with truth and power. This talent or gift is a large part of what I mean by creativity. It is there in all children, I feel, but it will not come to the surface unless it is recognised and encouraged.

In a discussion which lasted most of a morning, the children explained.

'Remember the "picture" poems? They were good.'

Of course this statement gave me no cause for delight, especially the past tense. What had happened to this form of expression, anyway? Why hadn't I encouraged that sort of writing? Again the children were directing us all back to this basis of thinking about values.

'I think "picture" poems are much like these shorter good things,' said Jennifer.

'Could they be turned into small poems?' asked Mary.

'Or could we just forget about them and write small poems and stories as we feel,' said Ron.

'And don't use our good thoughts, Ronny. Heck no!' said his sister.

'I didn't mean that at all. I meant that we shouldn't just try and say smart things.'

'You've been trying too hard Ron,' said Valerie. 'It comes easy if you don't try.'

The problem was indeed a big one, but we saw that small poems were really here to stay and would become a part of every week's writing as well as the basis of our recognition of the value of a piece of writing. The general value and architecture of a piece of writing eventually would be the final consideration of the papers presented, but the smaller statements of sincerity and meaning would be the 'stepping stones' to this understanding. I found always that I had to allow for the fact that the process of expression was one of generating a partial expression which demanded a fuller release. The selection of one group of ideas from an established individual's story, painting, pot, song, or drama can affect this sort of thing.

Sometimes I would work out part of a story for dramatization for the children to complete. I saw that the building up of expression was the extension of simple sincere thoughts into an expanded detail 'in depth'. It is enough to assist the child to recognise his good ideas and to encourage him to write further. I don't think we can help a child with his own ideas. That part is up to him. The most desirable situation which demands this release is that which the child himself creates. This is the point where many children will otherwise leave off working.

It seems to me also to be a basic principle of this form of education that we evaluate our work at regular points and go on when necessary to new points of expression. The children have to begin from something genuine and personal and come to realise it more fully or exactly during the expression. I had to see, too, that they might very well make a direct statement of some intensity that did not require further discharge.

Goldfinches feeding by Kathleen

118

9

TECHNIQUES TO ESTABLISH AWARENESS

A GREAT deal of the school work was directed towards establishing increasing attitudes of awareness in the children. Thus in art and poetry we had come to see that accuracy was an important part of the work and that it was in fact closely linked with the individual's awareness of his environment. I saw that there were all sorts of awareness, and much of the interest in creative work had to do with the differences in children in this respect. Some were observers of nature and showed a keener observation of scientific detail; others had a feeling for space relationships and noticed, for example, that a bird can fly within the bare branches of a winter tree. I think this awareness is also the basis of learning processes such as those found in arithmetic and spelling. There seems to be a close link between the discipline of observation and awareness in a science lesson, in painting, or in studying. I have often thought that proficiency in the formal school subjects might well be assisted by comparable disciplines in the 'expression' activities. The disciplines are no less important in either.

As a result of my belief in the value of the simple statement or image and its relation to every child's expression of ideas, I decided on a new attack in creative writing: expression as a result of studying a subject in considerable depth, from which the children would become so conversant with their subject that their expression would be spontaneous and intensely satisfying. I had seen how children's poems rarely extended past the simple image that to adult eyes would seem merely to be an idea for a poem. I did not think that either obscurity or expansiveness in the adult manner had necessarily to do with better poetry. I considered that child poetry, when it resulted from a study of the subject in considerable depth was good poetry.

In practice I had to devise means whereby intensity could be made evident, and for the purposes of this study I chose the subject of grass for the first experiment. A criticism could be made that I was using the children for my own ends; but I was not creating through the children, I was increasing their awareness in a way that might not otherwise have occurred to them.

Such statements as 'spider-elbowed grass' had been recorded. This of course came after some study of spiders and some of grasses. Finally we made a study of the form and function of a number of different grasses: tall fescue from the flood-plain drains, which grows six to eight feet high; bamboos in relation to common grasses; ryegrass and cocksfoot. These we studied in relation to various kinds of weather: rain in the grass and on it, wind over the long seed-heads, autumn on the hills, grasses on dull days, grasses on very hot, hot days. Up to this point there had been no indication that I wished the children to think and write about grasses especially. I usually have a writing period after or during each unit of nature study. In this investigation I did not give free time to thinking and writing as was usual, but I conducted the lesson myself. We took our papers and pencils out into the area where we had been working, and there we lay down and talked. Some started the inevitable pulling and tugging at grass heads, something children all over the world do. I asked them to write about the grass for the first time. I asked them what sort of grass it was. This implied that they could tell me what it did, and very soon in a matter of minutes all had written down a line or so.

GRASS

'Dry, tickling grass, wind-bent grass, long spiky and spotted grass, the weeded grass pointing out into the sun, flat-footed clover, rabbit's foot grass, foot-crashed grass, flattened to the grass, the tickled grass walked away into summer grass, brown, shivery eye, sheep tongued grass, sunburnt rye, dry chewing grass,' and so on.

None of these statements is remarkable, but I saw that already in a few words they expressed a feeling for the grass. Then I asked for some extension of this thought in the question, what does the grass do?

GRASS

'I saw the clip of the grass gently move. The long dry wind, bending ticklish grass. The sticky heat of the paspallum walk. The mown grass breath of the wind. The sharp needle of the prickly gorse sticking into grass tops. They sat and watched the blinking sheep and the long bent grass waves. The long silent grass blows over the hill. On the top of the hill is the grass bending over like me bowing.'

Here again was a certain feeling, but nothing that was not ordinary for these children. Many of the pieces began with 'I see', and there was a fair amount of repetition of similar ideas. Next I asked them all to lie down in the grass and look at it again. I did this for I believed that one of the principles of study of a subject in depth was that there were different ways of looking at the same thing. Chins to the ground for a moment, completely relaxed too, for a moment or two, but with studied concentration of the grass all the time—perhaps all we were doing was extending the 'range' of awareness of the environment by the bird's eye, worm's eye, cat's eye view, and so on.

GRASS

I lay down
I watched the tall bend of the trees.

                                    BRUCE

As the wind blows
The runaway grass
Hides beneath my feet.

                                    LIZA

The wind-bent grass
On the flattened,
Water-marked ground.

                                    RAYMOND

The cracked tree bark
Half peeled;
Slowly in the strange
Lighted sun.

                                    RAYMOND

I lie in the long grass
Watching the long, thin power pole
Through the tall seed headed grass.

                                    CLIFTON

As the silent wind blows
Across the lip of the hills
I see the grass bow
Against its mighty gale.

                                    JOHN M.

As I look through the grass
I see the girl's grass-shadowed dress.

                                    JOHN M.

As I was lying on my back
I heard the idgie-bidgies sing
Their thrilling music,
That made me dream I was a little insect.
When I woke up, the stalky sky
Was over my dreaming face.

                                    MAURICE, 8 years

When I looked through the brown seeded grass
I saw the wind waving.

                                    MAURICE

I see the short eaten grass
Away up on the gorse grassed hills.

                                    DENNIS

The grass breaking wind
That I have seen on the hills.

                                    MAURICE

I see the wandering wind
Tickling the cross shaped grass.

                                    DENNIS

I see the grass blowing
like white shadows.

                                    ERIC, 8 years

Another way of looking at grass was introduced to
the children when I asked them to look at far-away
things. This proved of great value to them, because it
allowed for new kind of poetic awareness. Nearly all the
children saw that the grass close at hand is far taller
than the hills or trees. The very situation was a poetic

one. We saw that we could investigate many new 'subjects' with the same creative inventiveness. My aim was to see how our awareness could be increased by examination of this 'subject' from as many points of view as possible.

GRASS

The paspalum seeds
That look like praying-mantis eggs
Which stick on long bowing heads.

RAYMOND

I saw the rolling leaves
Through the seed headed grass,
That were shivering away
Into the cracked branches,
Where tall brown grass
Was looking greedily at me.

LORNA

As I look at the brown bend of the trees,
The green brown leaves
Bow over the branches.

ERIC

As I lie in the long tall grass
I can see the flat fluffy clouds
Move slowly across the air
And the long, tall grass above.

RUDOLF

While I lie in the grass
I can see the seed-tipped grass

Touch the midday clouds.
As the grasshoppers and flies hop
From stalk to stalk,
I hear the crickets singing
and the cars speeding by.

JOHN

I lay down in the tall grass
That looked like paint brushes
in the sky.

BRUCE

I heard a fly buzz past.
I saw the thin string of a swing
Hanging down.
I saw a shining blackbird fly
With shining yellow beak.

MARILYN

I sat on the bow bent grass.
It waved over my body.
If I were only a fly
And the blue curved sky sat
Above me,
I could see the grasshoppers
Spring bone legs
Jump over me.

KENNETH

Finally, I asked the children to lie on their backs in the long grass and look up at the sky, and then write

123

again. The spell was broken for many, but four pieces were selected by the children for publication.

> I lay on my back.
> I could hear the idgie-bidgies
> Humming their beautiful song.
> Stilt long trees
> Flapped their beautiful brown bark.
>
> ERIC

> A little tiny, black ant am I,
> Crawling up a piece of spider-elbowed grass.
> I get on top of the thin topped stem,
> Where the giant sticky seed heads stick.
>
> DENNIS

> I lay on my back
> Stargazing at the brown bark trees
> That glim at my poor face.
> Idgie-bidgies singing their music song to me,
> Unhappy me.
>
> GLENNIS

> As I lay down in the grass
> I saw a branch of an oregon tree
> And I saw some clouds in the dark blue sky
> And I heard a noise and it was a cricket.
>
> KENNETH

These four poems are centred on the same situation and the children's consciousness of the cicadas is very apparent in three of them, even to a close approximation of the same words.

We repeated the process with a number of subjects, 'observing' and speaking our poetry. Then we painted some subjects, and for one we tried to explain our feelings in movement. 'Willows' was one study that we wrote about.

What sort of willows are they?

'Buoying willows, tide-dripping willows, eel-rubbed willows, leaf-dripping willows, Lent-leafed willows, thirsting willows, willow-rippling willows,' and so on.

This led on to these few poems which expressed complete ideas:

> The black cotton shag
> That dived before the willow roots
> From weeping green edged leaves.
> Soon blackness came up again.
>
> SONNY

> I saw the dead willow
> Floating down the drifting tide;
> It bobbed up and down like a turkey's head.
>
> ERIC

> As I look at the straining willow bough
> It makes me think it has been wrenched.
> Willows hang lazily drinking the acid water
> Hanging onto the bent bough.
>
> DENNIS

> I see the motionless river
> Drown the branches of the weeping willow
> The river slowly swells,

Even towards the overhanging branches of the willow.

JOHN M.

I see the sprinkled dangling water leaves,
Dangling water leaves,
Cool, and shake
Their willing leaves.

MARILYN

I feel that we had accomplished much in our examination of such subjects, and also we had discovered the principle of being aware of our environment. This is a valuable teaching technique, but also it is invaluable to the children as a basis of personal enjoyment for their life time.

Every time we embarked upon a new study, I first made sure that the topic was one which all wanted to work at. In this way we studied weeds, poplars, tree ferns, fences, pipi collecting, stone collecting, shells, and many others. In later investigations we gave the final aspects over to the individuals for their own kind of writing. Some wrote stories or prose, but most kept to poetry.

Mr Anton Vogt and I used this approach in work with teachers, and we were able to demonstrate that teachers could conduct personal discussion with children (as well as the class approach here described) and record their statements which later could be presented to the children concerned as the product of their own thinking.

The approach in this case was not the 'leading question one, for in no way was the answer put into the mouth of the child. This means of extending children was used by Mr S. H. S. Boyle, primarily as a remedial method, with children who had hitherto based their writings on teachers' models and teacher-chosen topics. As well, he used the method with beginners in the infant room (much the same way as Miss Raymond did in my own school) to bring out a story from paintings as the children completed them.

QUESTION	ANSWER
What is your painting about?	Magpies.
Do you like them?	I don't like magpies.
Why?	They taste awful.
Like what?	Like a terrible taste.
How terrible?	Like dog tucker.
Have you eaten one?	Yes.
Where did you get it?	I shot the magpie in the bush with my gun, dead, dead, dead.

Mr Boyle's work was designed at this time to assist children to became creative, but Miss Raymond's approach in our school was in some ways a step ahead of this, in that the children had come immediately into a fully creative 'atmosphere' and would tell their stories without any need to pose questions.

Some of the earlier writings of Clifton, Allan, and others are clearly fantasy statements: the throwing of a stone at a bird's bones; caterpillars hurting their teeth; and the blue sky sitting (in the same manner as Clifton) in the sky. Similar statements are heard from five and six-year-olds as they come to school for the first time:

'My centipede is called Beehunter and he has lots of hands to tickle me with: he has twenty-two hands. He lives under the house and eats dirt. He made his house himself and it isn't very good. His mother lives there too and her name is Sheema.'

DESMOND, 7 years

'Snowdrops are like little, little lights in a town at night time, only they would be in a very, very little town. Snowdrops are umbrellas for flies. They could be dresses for spiders and things like that.'

MONA, 7 years

All too soon these stories disappear as children become more impressed with the 'reality' of facts. At the same time there are many children who have never written or uttered such fantasy stories. However, all children are able to express their awe of the world about them. I was much impressed by a statement of D. H. Lawrence's in a newspaper article in which he said: 'The sheer delight of a child's apperceptions is based on *wonder;* and deny it as we may, knowledge and wonder counteract each other.' There were many indications at this time that much of the poetry of this school was indeed the expression of the child's wonder at this world Fantasy is a certain sort of imaginative feeling that all children should be free to express.

The success of the approach here was that children were encouraged to express their great sense of wonder, and even those children who had been maltreated from their earliest days could in time become engrossed in and excited about Desmond's centipede or Stuart's monkey. Adults who deny children the expression of their wonder and fantasy with insistence on factual statement and thinking are surely maltreating their children. The chapters on nature and social experiences show what children perceive through their senses (if they are allowed and if their work and thoughts have a favourable audience) but if the work in these 'subjects' were factual and scientific only I am sure (as Lawrence indicates) that there would be no expression of value to the child other than the repetition of many unfelt words. It was because of this knowledge and experience that we thought it necessary to allow for and encourage the expression of fantasy and wonder at a level that we had not known before.

Later I watched Stuart, a small boy in the infant room, show and tell with the twist and shaping of his small fingers all about the size and habits of a small insect that he had seen on a nature ramble:

'The flicky things were a dark colour, not black. They

Crab paintings, Jennifer

Roosters, oil painting by David N.

had little, little wings and long, long legs; they were so little nobody could see them—only me.'

Each wing, each leg was itself a thing that he had to explain with his bodily movements, and his painting of this delightful 'species' was also full of the same child excitement that his teacher quickly recognised. She wrote down the story and praised him for it. However, another person was there at the time, a person who was concerned that such a loose inaccurate description had been allowed to go unchecked.

'Was it an insect, Stuart?' he began. 'How many parts did it have to its body? Did it hop? Why do you say it was a 'flicky thing? Did it fly?' Of course there could be no answers. Stuart became more and more subdued, and when he was told to look more carefully in future when he was doing nature study, I saw that he was about to cry. 'The poor child,' I thought to myself; but this is just the way children have their natural feeling for fantasy and wonder driven out of them. At the age of five, and perhaps fifty-five, there is still a place for Stuart's sort of spontaneity. How often children can rise above such assaults on their imagination is not hard to guess.

I am sure that Lawrence did not mean that children should be without knowledge, but rather that there should be recognition of wonder and of knowledge, that one should not counteract the other, and as knowledge of such an insect grew so should the opportunities for expression grow.

Miss Raymond undertook to record all the stories over a long period and to hold regular discussions with the children. This meant that imaginative writings would be encouraged more and more. She began by recording everyday statements about their paintings, particularly in relation to new methods of story recording on the question and answer method as mentioned previously. Although she used questions to extend the statements of the children, she generally found that the stories and comments about the paintings flowed as fast as she could record them. The questions were kept as simple as possible, such as: where, when, how. The question and answer method is always of use with children who are unable to develop an idea and record for themselves adequately enough, and there are always a few who require this encouragement throughout their primary education. At the infant and lower standard level, however, the majority of the stories were those incidental to the day's activities. (Another proof that the child needs an opportunity to express his conflicts, aspirations, joys, and sadnesses.) At some time in the day children told stories to the recorder (not necesarily the teacher) so that most of the paintings had stories and most of the stories were painted.

The amount of work recorded was large, and by far the greatest amount of this was, as we would expect, the simple record of some happening or fact. Statements like 'Aunty's two dogs came to see us. Uncle and aunty came too.' 'Dad's shoes are too big for me' would be the sort of story that was actually written by a five- or six-year-old, whereas a long one like Kevin's was told to his teacher almost without prompting:

THE WEDDING

'We have got the drinks for Paul's wedding; there is orange and lemon and orange squash too. Last night we went up to Don's to get the turkey and when we got home, Teddy, Paul's mate helped us. We biffed the turkey in the wash-house and locked the door. We had made a bed of hay for it first. Tomorrow Lawrence and me might be allowed to get the axe and chop the heads off the hens and the ducks. Mummy will be going to cook them and some hens and some pork and five turkeys too. Paul's girl friend had long fingernails; boy they are long!'

KEVIN, 6 years

THE WEDDING

'Next morning we played with the gallon tins. We tied them on strings and threw them round and round our heads. When we got sick of tins we took fishing lines and went down to fish and Teddy and Kevin got eight eels. I didn't get so many but I wasn't trying hard. In the afternoon was Paul's wedding; everybody was very busy before it happened. Kevin said the best part was the drinks; he liked the orange fizz best. I liked the duck and the turkey. Paul got lots of presents; he got some beer glasses and a pirate on a horse with baskets and things for putting pepper and salt in that looked like apples.'

LAWRENCE, 7 years

'I caught a cricket and we put it on the nipper and they started fighting. Nippers are those things that nip you.'

TESSA, 5 years

'A bird was in our washhouse and it was trying to get through the window. Its wings were flapping and flapping and Mummy came and caught it and threw it out the window. Its wings went on flapping and it flew away.'

JEANETTE, 5 years

This experience so impressed us as a teaching group that we made further room for oral recording of stories in our programmes. This approach did much to lift the attainment of a number of children in the school who had been having difficulty in recording their simple stories. It remains a remedial method even at advanced stages of learning.

*   *   *

A second small group of writings was selected by the children as poetry. This selection was of course dependent on their knowledge of poetry from verse read (and painted as interpretations) in their short life at the school. Any element of child wonder was immediately called poetry. However, in 'This is Spring time because I can feel it and I know,' Desmond, 7 years, expressed a somewhat different feeling, but the children still called it

Cooking in the hangi (Maori oven), Lawrence, 7 years

poetry. Desmond didn't enter into this discussion, although soon afterwards he would specify whether his work was story or poetry.

'I saw trees swaying in the wind.
A bird came and perched.
I saw thistles with all their prickly heads on.
I saw all sorts of coloured barks and when I ran my finger along them, some were lumpy, some were just smooth.
The cold grass tickled my bare feet, like crackling ice I get out of the fridge.
I heard birds singing; I suppose they were happy. Sometimes I feel sad when someone dies.'

OLIVE, 8 years

'We saw a little tree in winter blowing over and Dad stamped it standing again.'

ERIC, 7 years

'Outside the bees are growling.'

STUART, 5 years

'I saw yellow and green ferns, looking like branches pointing out all ways out of little old trees.'

RYLAND, 6 years

'The grass looks like tiny tiny trees only littler.'

DESMOND, 7 years

Then there were fantasy statements:

'Last night we nearly found a star. We saw the star falling a long way down right out of the sky. It fell behind a post on our place and we ran to get it but we couldn't find it anywhere. We looked and looked all over the ground and still we could not find it anywhere. If we had found it we would have brought it to school to let you have a look and then we would have taken it home again just to keep.'

LAWRENCE, 7 years

'The river is dirty and muddy, all because the fish have been digging the bottom.'

DESMOND

'The river was very angry that it nearly cried.'

PETER, 6 years

'Wattle flowers are fluffy chickens that smell like nice soap.'

KEVIN, 6 years

'Santa Claus has things like spiders' webs on his face.'

STANLEY, 5 years

'I saw the milky way and it is just like a starry cloud.'

PETER

'Last night I caught the biggest eel and it has blue eyes and a white belly just like the pakeha.'

STANLEY

'The birds were flying looking for crumbs off the seeds. I would like to be a bird and lay big green eggs.'

MONA, 7 years

'I had a horse; one day he died. I don't know where he died—he just died on himself.'

STUART, 5 years

Such statements although common from Stuart, Kevin, Mona and Desmond were rarely seen from many of the

130   The fish digging in the river bottom, Desmond, 7 years

Monkey, spider and spider cage, Stuart, 5 years

others. We could only conclude that in the main the others were in need of this 'freeing up' process and to some extent some of the children did become fuller and more imaginative people.

The association of painting with story-making continued as valuable and highly interesting integration. Stuart's *Monkey and Germ* story and his painting (attributable in part to a lesson on cleanliness) was such a story.

'Our monkey died because he got germs. Germs are horrible to eat, because they have got mud all over them. My spider is all right. You can't see him because he is hiding. He is a big fat spider with legs all round; his eyes have prickly things on them to use on the rats. Once he found a germ thing and washed it and ate it.'

STUART, 5 years

Such fantasy statements of little children appear naturally, but with older children who have not known any encouragement of their imaginative ideas it was a different matter. At first it seemed that it might be wrong to expect fantasy from older children, but when the class magazine of the younger children's work was first presented for reading by the older children of the school the enthusiasm for every aspect of it indicated that they identified themselves with this kind of thinking. In a discussion all claimed that they thought to themselves in fantasy at some time, but one in seven said that they did not often think in this manner.

As far as poetry thinking was concerned I was impressed that Jennifer, Glennis, Sonny, and Marilyn claimed that many of their thoughts were poetry whereas the rest said they only thought in poetry sometimes. Thus every child claimed a familiarity with imaginative thinking. I believe that this indication by the children about their frequency of thinking in these ways would probably be true enough, allowing for some confusion as to definition of fantasy and wonder.

Statements of wonder seem associated with children always:

'It's raining, but the world will be round tomorrow.'

'I try to catch the clouds on the hill, but when I get there they are gone.'

It seemed reasonable, in view of the lower school question-and-answer approach, to begin with the senior children on that basis, too. I asked simple questions which required at first a scientific or real answer if that was possible. Why is it raining? All had answers, few of which had any real value as an answer to the question. But when I asked for a second answer to the same question, one that would be the fantasy answer (or wonder for that matter) the answers were enlightening.

'The sun sucked the water from wells, buckets and creeks and when it was full it rained.'

KINGSLEY, 11 years

'Rain dripped all through a wet night and wet footprints were walked through the house.'

JOHN, 11 years

What is wind?

'The light green grass that covers the hills.' 'It wavers white-faced people in the sky.'

CLIFTON, 10 years

'Papers on the table: There was no sun, only wind.'

GLENNIS, 9 years

There was thus a wide range of 'interpretation', and I saw that the exercise appeared to assist the children to a greater understanding of themselves. We went on to a great deal of 'fact and fantasy' writing, which became valuable in discussion of serious prose where fact is important.

Shortly afterwards we had to revert to personal expression. For a period the programme had to be unbalanced in favour of the new approach until most or all of us felt the 'rightness' of the new extension. We had to feel that wonder and fantasy were an important part of our thinking and writing. This is a principle of concentration that I believe is important in creative teaching; for when the children get on with their own personal thinking and expression, they do so with greater understanding of themselves and the world about them. The exercise of answering questions allowed for the 'settlement' of the *freedom* which enlarges our means rather than 'colours' all our expression.

The work went on.

'I saw the river eels turned into weeds at the bottom.'

RUDOLF, 9 years

'Thistles with annoying spikes.'
'Wading in the paddocks.'

DENNIS, 10 years

'The reflection of the puddle burns.'

LORNA, 9 years

'The laughing fridge is smart. I'm going to give it the works.'

GLENNIS

When the time for freedom from this exercise approach came, I noted several things: A few children went on with work left off at the onset. Many continued with small fantasy ideas and produced pages of short poems, many of which seemed to have an almost metaphysical quality. Some wrote poems of simple but intense quality, which in many cases resembled oriental poetry in expression of beauty. A few wrote what appeared to be **rubb**ish, and others painted and illustrated descriptive dreams and fantasy experiences.

Examples of poems in which fantasy is paramount.

EARTH

The earth turns around
Like a ripple
And swings
Through moon-space.

BRUCE, 8 years

CLOVER

Clover lies still,
Like the clouds
In the blue quilt of my bed.

MARILYN, 8 years

STICKS

Dead burnt sticks in the swamp
Sticks from the stars.

CLIFTON

SHELLS

Shells mimicking the sea;
A storm battering the trees.

DENNIS, 10 years

STARS

Cats' eyes
Twinkled from the sky.

SONNY

FLAMES

The flames licked across the fern;
Pottery in the kiln.

ERIC, 11 years

THISTLES

I saw thistles noses sniff with cold.

RUDOLF

STARS

I said to myself
I could jump and get
One of them stars.

BRUCE

Statements in which better observation of the environment is recorded:

THE RIDGE

'A ridge made of light green hills dotted with many specks of white. A brown tuft of rushes there tough and straight. The prickle green of the gorse bush with little bunches of yellow; the blackened stalk of the teatree with seeds like bells. And in the branches is a bird: the flash of his wings, his fluttering tail. His feet laid back in the wind.'

TONY, 12 years

DEW

'Little drops of dew glisten like diamonds and light the power lines with little lights that roll down the wire like marbles. A sparrow lands and shakes the lights off and the few left grow brighter as the sun comes out, flicking off and on like traffic lights when the wire moves.'

KENNETH, 10 years

Verses in which poetry is strong in contrast to fantasy.

SUN

The blue faded sky
Blinded the grassheads.

GLENNIS

SUN 2

The sunshine beneath the water
That made a petal.

GLENNIS

RIVER 2

The stars are lost
Hiding under the water,
The moon is drowned.

JENNY

PINE

Red leaves of the pine tree
Floating in the after-tea sky.

LORNA

WHIRLPOOL

The whirlpool showed me
The picture of the sky.
The boulders showed their way down
The bottom of the river.

ERIC

Shags drown in the sky,
Legs hang on the moon.

JENNY

WILLOW

A green willow floats on the water
Little boats drift in a whirlpool
and sink in the sky.

CLIFTON

NIGHT

The stars hide in the cattle drains
The moon prowls
By a blue spiked leaf.

JENNY

135

RIVER

The fish scales sparkled in the water
Stones scraped over the clouds.

JENNY

RUSHES

The wiwi brushes the low clouds.
Fluff with water dripping
on spiky bits of clouds.

LORNA

GRASS

Green grass
Like the grass in my painting:
Green in the top of the trees;
Blue through the spaces.

CLIFTON

EVENING

The sky is dull
The stars are with the birds.

GLENNIS

The improved observation of everyday happenings led us at this stage to record directly many aspects of our surroundings. It appeared that the experience gained in broadening our expression with fantasy writing did assist in observation and thinking about the environment.

It's amazing that such big hills
Grow in such little puddles.

TONY

The pool was shallow,
Hills were covered.

CLIFTON

Frogs choked:
Sewered puddles in the bottom;
Glass broke in the pond.

GLENNIS

The birds fly fast, turning their beaks to the morning star.

BRUCE

Morning whistled the song of a blackbird.

CLIFTON

Flying stringy winds were high in the sky.

LORNA

A puff of dust on the road,
Sparrows dust bath.

TONY

MORNING

Light edged flame spread over the country side.

BRUCE

A kingfisher on the power line: the quickening flash of wings; a worm from the ground.

TONY

Thistle down walks so slowly pulling mist from a hole.

BRUCE

The river glided around a bend under my feet:
It crouched low under a log; it snored to itself
As it ran over sharp stones;
It cuddled up under the water lilies,
Sucking them away;
It was famished for eely bait.
The sopping willows danced over their drink.

MAURICE, 8 years

The dark shape of a bird flashed from shade to
    shade.

TONY

I crouched under a trunk,
A low flying bird settled.

GLENNIS

The grounds were empty and the only moving thing
    was
The wind blown grass and a flying tree.

CLIFTON

The cracks in the ground swallow the crickets.

CLIFTON

The frightening of a flower:
Bees muscles singing.

GLENNIS

Oiled feathers were splattered with rain
As white seagulls came in from the sea.

JOHN, 10 years

A squeaky throat charmed the air.

DENNIS

I saw that this work drew the children nearer to so many common things about them; nearer to observations of pure poetry in their environment. I felt that all of them could approach their work more imaginatively. Thus Glennis, who was studying the leaf and spine impression marks on a giant *Agave americana*, wrote a small poem which in part is fantasy thinking.

THE GARDEN

The garden stands alone, with cactus, rushes and
    stones around the edge
Little marbles sit on the rushes.
Sandflies crawl up the straight edged path;
Little trains spiked out with smoke roaring out;
Slime drizzles down the cactus from a snail that
    has lost its way
Bees hummed their way for honey.
Little birds hopped along the path
beside the lonesome garden.

GLENNIS

As the normal expression work went on, Eric wrote a short piece about telephone poles and wire, and Jennifer began a fantasy lino-cut of a crab. This led her on to write her fantasy, and the satisfaction associated with this 'energy discharge' led her to a full and complete visual statement of fantasy crabs.

TELEPHONE POLES AND WIRE

'Noise was soft and sweet; a bird was living and singing in the wooden pole. Millions of sirens came closer

137

Crab by Jennifer

from the cities as voices clicked down the pole. The wind swept over the wires and they sang sweeter than the river, softer than the river.'

ERIC

CRABS

'The untidy crabs scuttled around the rocks; sometimes they turned upside down and lay there like shining stars in the sky. Their little blue nippers were like twisted barbed wire and some of them looked like an evening frock. The little dead white one was a light-hard limpet. The tough scales on their backs were like toenails for they ate fish's scales to get hard backs. They scuttled under rocks like thunder clouds rolling across the sky. The ones with brown on were like dead autumn leaves. Some of them looked salty. I wonder who threw the table salt over them?'

JENNY

I was indeed pleased to see so much good craftsmanship come out of the fantasy experience, but the stimulation of sentences such as:

'Some of them looked like buttons,' 'The big one with a purple back was a brooch which stuck on to an evening frock,' and 'They scuttled under the rocks like thunder clouds rolling across the sky,' were so thought provoking that they became subjects of separate paintings by Jennifer.

In this work I saw some of the better possibilities of integrated expression in art and crafts, and from that time the paintings too became far more imaginative. The lino print of Marilyn's *Thrush Flying* and Jennifer's *Dance Figures* are representative of this development.

In all these various language 'expansions' that we experienced over the years I became increasingly aware of a simple process of absorption of the freedom to express. I believe the approach to extending language expression to be creative in itself. Certainly for a time

Large fantasy crabs by Jennifer

Thrush flying by Marilyn

such investigations cut across the general line of personal expression (and this should as a principle, be avoided) but when the 'discoveries' were over and work returned to what may be called 'normality', the whole personality of expression was enlarged, and in many cases it allowed the children to see themselves as people in their environment more clearly.

The amount of integration possible is always reduced while such an experiment is under way, but the ultimate integration is always so much more valuable and intense. The case of the paintings and craft work of Jennifer and others supports this statement. The usual and personal statements in any field are full and satisfactory and are not related to possible artificial situations of 'discovery'.

I believe Glennis's *Birds at Night and Day* to be an honest expression of ideas which could not be expressed as adequately by Glennis in any other way.

Two groups of dance figures by Jennifer

BIRDS AT NIGHT AND DAY

'When I am asleep a dream comes like a nightmare's face. The scales of a nightingale sit on the branch, in the house with river peeping noises. A nursery bird and a doctor bird and sick children come and sit beside the nightingale.

'I think I can watch them when the night is done and the day has come. Me, getting out of bed and feeling around the branch for the nightingale and the other birds on the boundary. Noises have gone and fingered feathers have finished flapping the daylight away. The windows are pale and the dark has gone to England. The Maori face has gone, that ghost was ragged and rude with no mouth, but my nightingale wasn't. I would like to see one.'

GLENNIS

It is interesting to look back some three years to a story written by David W., then aged 11 years. This story called *Three Hills* is an imaginative fantasy story in which David withdraws from the dangers and substitutes Hori at regular intervals. His story was written years before we began this later work, and even though we all admired the 'magic' quality of his story the secret of this success remained his. In this and many other aspects of creative adventure David has led others.

The three hills by David W.

THE THREE HILLS

'The three hills stand still and are shrewd. At the back of the third hill a stream flows strongly and in the stream is a fat black, hairy eel which has two big, sharp, intelligent eyes and it lives in a stoned hole that goes down and never ends.

'At the first of these hills there is a black stinking boy called Hori; he lives under the shadow of the first hill where the dark sounds live.

'At the second hill, where nothing can be destroyed, where six olden stones lie, is a dog which is the neighbour to Hori.

'And next to the dog is the hill called the third hill and there as I said before in that hole lives the magic eel which can stare at anything, the magic eel that can change into anything it likes.

'One day, Hori, the boy took his spear to fight the eel; the spear was long and the end was sharp. I pity the black eel, I said this to myself as I looked at the sharpened jagged end of that spear.

'At about noon I set off with Hori to fight the magic eel. Across the two hills is a long way to go, and coming to the second hill, I can't go anywhere where the dog lives so Hori shouted out to the dog "Paru, paru, paru" (come here dog) and the dog came out and went with the boy, for the dog knew what the boy was trying to do. It wasn't long before the boy and the dog came to the third hill and there was the stream where the magic eel lived and just by the hole was the eel feeding by the water's edge where the weeds grew. But he saw the boy and shot into the hole but came out again as the ugly man was saying drily as could be, "What's the meaning of trying to spear me?"

'The ugly man stood still and his eyes looked at the ground and I saw that he was brown skinned and wild looking, his ears stuck out and up to a point and his hair was dirty and black coloured even his chin came to a point and when he looked at me I couldn't look back because he looked such a sight. He was magic and strong so I would not fight him, I turned my head away and started to walk away from the ugly man who was an eel that lived in the stream. He was a cruel man, of course, his nose was skinny and his mouth was sharp.

'The boy shuddered and slid his feet backwards from the jagged entrance to the hole, where the water weeds spring back and up in the current, that comes from the hole that goes down and never ends. And the boy, Hori, shuffled away from the hole on the third hill as the ugly man came towards him.

'The boy was terribly frightened of the brown rumpled skinned man who came shaking towards him with the black chipped knife pointing out the heart of the black eyed boy. The boy who raised his pigeon spear at the ugly man and who sent it through the ugly man's blood thirsty heart; and as the ugly man lay groaning on the ground, horribly he groaned as he died . . .

'Hori climbed down the Ugly Man's hole from stone to stone, down the hole that has no end and as he came to where the imps were he saw paintings which told him what to do and they told him wrong things; and there were paintings which turned him away with horror; they were of dead men and some others were horrid designs and while Hori was looking at them he heard strange noises and on the wall a hand just started to move quickly and Hori, frightened, ran further down the hole. And all of a sudden he met a shoal of imps.

'He stopped so suddenly that all he said was, "You are . . . the imps." And the boy in the end asked the imps for power but the imps said that they had no power for him. "We have only our own power and we can't give any away and we shall kill you unless you go away for a message has come to us and it tells us to send you away." And the boy ran up the stoned stairs as fast as his legs could carry him; he ran past the stairs where the horrid pictures moved on either side of him and as he ran up the hole he could hear the noises running after him and behind him and they were the imp noises that frightened him.

'And the boy came out of the hole with horror and fear and soon he came to the ugly man and he pulled his spear out of his wild heart and the wild man jumped up and half cursed and gave the boy a whelting punch and

143

the boy fell deadly on the ground, but soon he rose again and ran away for his life and the ugly man stopped to see where the boy went and he saw that he had gone to the third hill and before the ugly man could get to his hole the boy Hori was on his way to talk to the imps again, and he was asking them to help him, help him? . . .

'The ugly man found that he could not go down the hole and that he got all wet and covered with weeds as he tried. He was waiting for the boy at the entrance to the hole and when he came out he caught the boy by the neck: "I'm going to kill you", he said and he pulled his bunch of knives out and he killed the boy and he took the boy's wealth but he pulled the knives out and the boy got up again and when he was right up they fought and fought for hours and hours and the blood was everywhere and the knives were in full action and the chips from the blades were buzzing everywhere and the blood thirsty men fought four hours more and their veins were watering the grass and the grass turned red, because the blood was raining on the grass.'

DAVID, W., 11 years

Native dancer, Dennis W.

144

10

SOCIAL STUDIES

I was biased towards craft and painting in history and geography studies such as in Neville's Polynesian canoe and Varley's study of ancient man. I saw that crafts and model-making were very valuable to the children, but at the same time I was dissatisfied with some aspects of this work. The printing of a tapa cloth sail with a lino block did not seem closely related to the real experience of making a tapa sail from plant material, nor did the gouging of a limb with gouges and chisels seem closely related to the actual experience of burning and chopping charcoal from wood. I felt that the verbal statement of knowledge was not as full as it should be, but I knew that the children understood their studies far better now that I had introduced the making of models and painting activities.

Playing with these models, such as the launching of Neville's canoe in the river with involved elements of improvised drama and imaginative talk, was a valuable experience in which I noticed more expression of the feeling of native village life than had come out of the written work. The launching gave added meaning to a section of work that many would have had difficulty understanding. This experience allowed me to see that though model making and a liberal use of arts and crafts was important, drama provided deeper meaning. When the children produced short plays on some social experience they displayed their real understanding in their own terms. Thus I found that drama, especially when a narrator carried the story in a kind of drama-mime, was full of the many impressions gathered in the process of living in the school and home. The drama showed me how deeply the children had absorbed the knowledge of their studies. I realised the relative 'shallowness' of the children's grasp of reality in relation to many social experiences. Yet I felt that drama offered a means of translating certain things into meaning for the child in the same way as crafts and art did.

Children readily make a choice of the media of their expression. They seek an outlet for their creativity and choose the most adequate way of expressing their feelings. In this they are influenced by people around them, and as my knowledge of drama was not great the children tended to choose crafts and painting. I was in fact holding back the development of their dramatic expression. I was later to learn that dramatic experiences helped the children to go on to language expression that was most meaningful.

Much of the social experience of local history described here was introduced through stories which were dramatized first in small sections then in complete plays. The adventures of drama and movement were not enough by themselves, and the stimulation of one expression (in each case after drama and story) led to another. In this way painting and crafts were used, and then creative writing. All children relate the study to their own real knowledge of their own environment.

Varley, Nell, and Kelvin began the language work when they wrote poems and accounts of the massacre of the ship's company of the trading ship *Boyd* in Whangaroa Harbour, which we visited at that time.

HOW THE MAORIS ATTACKED THE BOYD IN 1809

Fluttering in the wind
Came in the *Boyd*,
Full sail ahead.
That night a Maori boy
Stole away to the chief.
The chief said, 'Utu.'
That night paddles dipped.
Canoes came whispering out
To kill for utu.*

VARLEY, 14 years

THE SORROW OF THE BOYD

The sorrow was all unexpected
The Maoris had all 'patued'†
The poor old captain Flogem.
They were all friendly,
Or they tried to be.
The Maoris were all too wild
You could not stop them.
Neither lion nor tiger.
Angry they were,
Nothing to stop them.
He pulled the trigger and bang went the jigger,
The spark flew out
Right onto the powder
And boooom, up went the ship.
That was the end of the poor old chief.

KELVIN, 9 years

THE BOYD

'The people on the little boat that killed the good Maoris were very foolish people, they were not wise, they were foolish.

'Foolish people do not do the right thing all the time, they mostly do the wrong thing and do not obey God, which is a bad thing.'

NELL, 8 years

* 'Utu' means the price to be paid.
† A 'patu' is a short flat weapon.

146

'The *Boyd* was a nice boat but the people on it were not nice at all. I would not like to be the Maoris. It was not a nice life for the fighters. If I were a Maori I would swat them in the eye.'

NELL

THE BOYD

The *Boyd* she came in with a sailor Maori boy,
Who'd been flogged with knotted rope.

That night he got off that boat and went to tell
the chief
This shocking affair.
The chief said, 'We'll have *utu*.'

After dark that Xmas night all the good warriors
Got their patus and waddies and got up to have *utu*.

After killing for *utu*, an old warrior playing with
a musket
Let a spark into a barrel and blew up the ship.

Floating up the harbour went the *Boyd* exploding
and burning
And landed at an island just leaving ribs above the
waterline.

Whale boats came and killed the good who tried
to protect the *Boyd*
Those poor Whangaroa Maoris and careless
whalers.

VARLEY

In this aspect of our work many stories from the history of the North were studied. One of these concerned the Maori pa, Taratara, one of the strongest natural sites for a pa in the Whangaroa harbour. It was here that a great siege occurred in which repeated attacks were beaten off and the pa taken only after it had been evacuated. The story is almost a folk-tale in these parts and concerns Hone Heke the leader of the attackers and the Ngapuhi tribesmen of Taratara. We never found out how much of the story was true, but as the children returned and re-told the story as grandfather told it or as mother said it happened a set of basic facts was assembled. If the fairies of nearby Motunehunehu Pa made the steps with footprints on them from the sea up to the Pa above (and they are certainly convincing looking steps and footprints) then perhaps there is a core of Taratara tragedy that really did happen. Round this story weeks of work centred. In the versions of the story related by the children, the most dramatic and interesting elements were seized upon.

'The screams of the old women and children, who were thrown over the cliff to the rocks below, that was horrible,' said Michael.

'But Hone was wild because the defenders had deserted and so avoided his vengeance. Remember he had made several attempts to storm the pa and each must have cost many warriors,' said Mary, whose grandfather knew the pa and the story well. When poems on the story were written, Christopher remembered this and wrote:

And he saw the bones of dead men
Lying at the foot of the pa,
Some were stuck into the ground
Like branches.
'The cannibal feast, how horrible!'

'And the warriors creeping through the bush in the early morning mist, that must have been a good part of the story,' said Nell.

The children were so interested in the man Hone Heke that at the outset they wanted to hear the full story of his life, through all his wars to his final burial in some far and secluded cave in the ranges that we could just see from Oruaiti. They also enjoyed the stories of Hongi, his uncle, and while the classroom echoed to the dramatization of the beginnings of the Taratara Pa battle, the playground was the scene of many battles between 'Governor Grey's men' and 'Hone Heke's warriors'.

Children demand this broadening of their knowledge and are full of questions about the characters or things connected with the story. During the two or three days when the story versions were related there were many discussions on parts of the story, many pictures were painted, and study of things like Maori war-clubs or battle-dress was undertaken. This knowledge became personal to each child and laid the foundations for expressive work to follow. All this discussion and study is most important for it raises the feelings and knowledge of the children to a level above the mere facts of the story where they can be easily related to and used for expression in the arts, language, movements, and drama.

After these beginnings it was suggested that the story might be acted. And so the drama was planned. But since a day contains only so many hours the first part of the story alone was fully developed. The first plan and approach to the attack was discussed, sections of the story were written or worked out by groups, parts were studied, and there was a great deal of rehearsal. Some of the aspects dealt with were the following: the situation of the pa, the spies looking out over the land, creeping through the fern, early morning in the swamp, the warriors coming through the raupo swamp while the wild ducks and pukekos were calling out, and creeping through the fern in the gully by the school to study the noises made.

After the play was over and the story was being recorded, Jennifer and Valerie wrote of these preparations in their poems.

Through the strangling and dusty ferns,
The warlike tribe of Maoris crept
While white lines of musty fog
Drooped down from the stillness of the trees' leaves
And pushing hands, stinging eyes and cold legs
Moved quickly through the whispering raupo

Dance mime, warriors in the flax

And the white tail of a pukeko spy flew up
To the morning mist of the soggy swamp beyond.

Pukekos squealed and drifted to some other place
    in the swamp,
Ducks clicked their beaks and woke the morning
    fog,
A stick cracked as a blood thirsty warrior
Crept up the hill,
A weka scuttled to the protection of the pallisades,
A stone rolled down the hill,
And someone climbed the watch tower.

THE PLAY

At last the play 'The Siege of Taratara' was ready, and Mary the narrator began.

'At the head of the Whangaroa Harbour, across the wide covered mudflats, through the cloaking mangroves that line the shores, up the winding river in the shelter of outstretching mangrove branches, the war canoes of Hone Heke came in the dark of a moonless night. Even to the foot of the raupo swamp, where the bitterns call and the pukekos creep, they came.'

Owen led his warriors from their canoes, which were covered carefully and quietly in raupo leaves. Mary continued, 'A morepork called from the scrub of the firm ground beyond, and a pukeko squealed near at hand, and the call of the night hunting kiwi was heard from the bush. Then through the mud and water of the swamp the line of battle-dressed warriors waded, and as the ducks rose from their nests and secluded pools and winged across the mists of early morning below Taratara pa the men reached the shelter of the manuka and taraire trees. The fern lay beyond the patches of blade-rattling flax, and up high the dark shape of the pa loomed where surely watchers were standing by the walls and watch towers.'

Within the pa sleepers stirred in their huts, while the cries of disturbed ducks flying by caused some of the guards to mumble and peer carefully into the dark.

So the play went on. The enemy without was sighted and battle commenced. The defenders rolled boulders down the slope, and the rumbling sounds were faithfully reproduced till this first attack was driven off. Hone Heke retreated. The occupations of the pa then recommenced: the kumara planting, the digging of fern roots, spearing of pigeons, the young Maori girls singing down the path to the water springs.

Finally when the next assault came the pa defenders quietly slipped down ropes and vanished into the bush. Owen's warriors found the gates open, and a few old women and children within.

The fire and fire noises as the pa burnt were acted by the defenders as the conquerors dragged imaginary bodies away to what Barbara called the 'awful hangi'.

The play was completed in its first 'draft' and had to be re-written a number of times. Anna asked to be

Hangi at Taratara by David W.

narrator one time and Nell another. As each version was finished small comments on parts of the play were made. 'I liked the children gathering wood for the early morning fires,' said Ted. 'And the "tattling of cabbage trees talking" was good,' said Anna. These comments and the poetry of the drama gave birth to the idea of producing a narrative poem on Maori life and the attack on a pa together with an 'awful hangi'. David W. began a large wood-cut at once.

The play had now reached the stage where careful consideration of its contents could be made without distracting or spoiling the children's enthusiasm for the production. For this I thought the movement of the warriors in the swamp or the throwing and rolling of boulders would be good starting points, but I knew that the children would have their own ideas and, for example, might consider the crawling through the bush and fern a much better one. These points of departure for movement had no direct connection with the play, except that whatever was done would certainly have an influence and bring about more imaginative movement in the sequence of the drama. However, there was only one reason for isolating these sequences, and that was so they would make very enjoyable developments in movement.

The sound of the warriors' legs in the boggy swamp, the calling and noise of flight of startled birds, and the simulation of wind in the bull-rushes with the attendant movements had been the best part of the play. But the boulder-rolling and throwing was open to much improvement. So in twos or threes we rolled large rocks to the parapets and hurled them down the cliff. 'The warriors' raised rocks above their heads and hurled them down. All sorts of heavy weights were rolled, tilted, heaved, pitched, and tossed. Many creeping and crawling movements, too, were devised and experimented with. These 'lessons' dealt with movements of two kinds: the interpretative and the abstract. The first movements meant something in terms of the play and were not done for their own sake. However, when free abstract movement to a simple drum rhythm was started at the end of the lesson, some of the interpretative movements were expressed in an un-verbal and abstract way. Previous to any of this movement the children analysed many small movements in a series of 'exercises' as in a physical education lesson. I am sure that anyone can help children enjoy any movement or game or even strict four lines drill because children naturally love movement itself; but success in the unrelated and formal approach to movement, although spontaneously accepted by children as good fun, is felt to be an incomplete answer to movement in its relation to living. This complete form of abstract movement was intellectual movement, and children are not intellectuals; besides the joy they get through expression in bodily movement they are concerned with the functions of all aspects of living, as their work in drama indicates so well. In the same way as they see their design work as a function of their pottery decoration, they feel their movement is a function of their drama and mime, and so movement has become more interpretative in nature. Perhaps the reason for the lack of success of some teachers in special forms of creative expression is the isolation of their subject by a process of intellectualization. Movement, in the intellectual way, becomes merely a consideration of the many elements in and numerous ways of expression through the fingers, hands, arms, legs and trunk without any link to nature, people, or drama.

In the same way as elements from the drama of Hone Heke were used as the basis for explorations in movement, the noises of the swamp, the birds, the wind, the water were used as sound pictures and co-ordinated into a complete auditory play. The sound stories were much the same as the play: the canoes coming up the river and startling the mute herons and the gulls. The finale with the dying screams and moans of the kuia (old women) as they were thrown to their deaths was most impressive.

These sound pictures are closely related to the beginnings of music. The five-line staff and the octave seem to be quite unchildlike. The picture-sounds that the children made have been used with percussion instruments, with movement alone, and with drama and poetry. Children's music is much simpler than the adult conception, but naturally the adult form is part of the heritage of the young.

The children did write simple songs using the five-line staff, using A to G names or other notations of their own. These songs were sung with the orchestra of drums and several other instruments. The triangles were recognizable. The other instruments had yet to be named. The song-writing and song-singing did not seem to be the whole of music. Occasionally there was a tie-up with the rhythm of natural sounds and movement that fired us with excitement, but which we lost when we tried to grasp it. Besides these occasional attempts we failed to make music fully creative.

*   *   *

The environment of the valley has always been the starting point of digressions into history and geography of this and other lands. From the story of Hone and Hongi and their wars began a study of the everyday life of a pa, and although the poetry narrative of Hone Heke's fight was well advanced, in the end a new poem was completed. Some of the verses of his poem were chanted to a drum accompaniment, others were read to the singing of Maori songs, and a few were shouted as hakas.

The suspicious morning,
The morning was quiet and peaceful
But froze in a thick whirling string of mist.
In the far away hills little glowing patches of rising
    sun
Crept higher
and higher
Into the sky.

153

The pukekos by David W.

The rustling of raupo
And a squawk.
A pukeko was disturbed and yet another.
Everything was camouflaged
But seemed to move
In a strange way
Towards the pa.

RONNY

Soon the sun came up
Flooding the frosted stones
Making them shine

Casting shadows on the ground
From the little twigs.

VALERIE

And said Ronny, a Maori boy in a chant of near
despair:
I was the first warrior,
I got the worst of everything.
The frozen stiff scrub
Scratched about my body like a gorse patch
And I took the blame for all the show
That was given away,
My eyes stung, stung with the filthy dust
That rose in the wind
From the dusty fern.
The mist swerved and spliced about the pa
And made things hard for me to see.
The call of birds made everything seem suspicious
Then a sudden splint of flame went whirling
Over the well-watched walls of the sleeping pa
And the smoke crept high
From the burning raupo houses.

RONNY

The tall spikes of the Maori pas dotted the horizon,
The wind whistled through the towering pallisades
 surrounding them,
And the watch towers could be plainly seen above
 the pallisades.

MAVIS

154

Soon a red glow rose over the Eastern hills
And mist settled on the trees and bushes about the
    pa
And children climbed through the traps
And ran for sticks.

VALERIE

Understanding was obtained through detailed study of local pa sites, and several large, detailed pictures were used for talks and lessons. We discussed the best way of fortifying a nearby hill, and we planned attacks and repulses in our drama. Mavis's and Valerie's poetry is a simple expression of their feeling for the subject. The children climbing through the traps to get the kindling wood is related to the simple job many of the children here have to do every night in the valley. Valerie's lines are an effective indication of her identification with our work.

Subsequently we studied the development of the valley during the hundred years' settlement by the white man. Through this investigation, which continued as the framework for all studies of man and other things, various modes of creative expression were exploited: dramatization, thought- or impression-writing, which is a good means of realising the absolute meaning in terms of our own lives, poetry narrative-writing, prose story-writing of equivalent lives in time or place. With these the arts and crafts have been used to the full. Certain children who do not readily express themselves in words seem to be better suited to model-making, through which, however, they often verbalize quite considerably on the subject under study. Model-making without an attempt at verbalizing has proved to be inadequate. The arts made it possible for them to say something, often in a surprisingly satisfactory way, which could not be said before. The great strength of all creative expression is that, when it is given scope in one suitable medium by some process of mind, this creative expression is transferred to another medium in which formerly there has been no proficiency. In passing, it might be useful to mention another stimulus to good creative writing: when new work is planned, the enthusiasm generated by research into new books, new directions in drama, painting, and crafts creates a certain tone which lifts the work of all. For example, in some of the verses written for the narrative poem about the white settlement of the valley, even children of moderate ability excelled.

The night was cold and dark
And the wind hummed and whistled through the
    straight pallisades
Spits of rain splashed and dripped on the walls
And thunder crackled and rumbled in the far hills.

RONALD

And the battered seagulls glided from heavy heavy
    shores
The wild cries were heard of Maoris from the
    beaten shores

155

And the heavy rolling of stones
The lonely shore rolled with stones
Polished, bright chipped and smooth stones.

VALERIE

And through the dark caves of olden Maoris
The skulls and bones of man-clubbed
Hung around the walls.

CHRISTOPHER

The gathering clouds on a winter's day grew black
And from far away peaks rain like mist
Hung hungrily upon the tall mountains
Rumbling, roaring and rattling.

The thunder pounded upon
The Maori houses
The wind whistled and waved itself about
Hung high up in the air
And sprang down
At the Maori raupo rustling houses.

SARAH

And so another drama, another narrative poem, and associated lino-cuts and paintings were started. The inclusion of Christopher's short poem is in itself an example of the way in which an individual, in his enthusiasm for a major work, can contribute something that would have normally been beyond his ability.

The sun set down below the far away hills
The fires blazed and twirled upward into the sky
And pink and yellow ran like ink across the piece
   of paper
And streaked like the river
Running over stones.

VALERIE

The last word of the story was told with a mark of satisfied completion, an element all too commonly neglected in creative works. Things must be clear in their definition, and it is important that there is the correct and firm termination. The length of one day, from first early light to evening and the time of sleep, has been repeatedly used with great satisfaction in our drama, stories, and poetry. A play or story could just as easily end in sleep or a halt for a rest, but no matter what it is, it is important that the end should be felt.

156

Fern design by Michael

11

NATURE STUDY

NATURE study began with rambles. We studied things as we came upon them, and this proved to be the best approach to this work for we could go back and see the changes at various times in the year. This work led us to satisfactory beginnings in lino cutting and painting and then on to writing. Observation, discussion, experimentation, and expression followed in almost every study we made, and this was the basis of our programme.

There were, however, studies that began in unusual ways, perhaps beginning from some interest of an individual; one such study was that of wasps. The children were making balsa wood, bamboo, and cane models, using various coloured plastics to provide the coloured light. The sun streamed into the room, but for a time it became weaker and the children who were trying out the models for their projected light on to white sheets of paper had to stop and wait. Attention wandered until again the sunlight flooded the room. The light faded and brightened several times. Children walked around the room going about various tasks: Clifton was making a number chart and a model for the addition of fractions, Lewi was doing a set of simple addition sums, and Eric was copying a story of his on to a stencil for the magazine. Eric looked up, walked over to the window, and returned to his seat. I watched him for a while as he looked into space in the room, and then I saw him go over to the window and look at an apple core that was placed on one of our best pots. Then I saw that he had been watching wasps. He checked off the few insects on the windows and wandered back to work.

'All workers still, but it won't be long now,' I heard him say to Necia, his sister. This was the beginning of our wasp study, which occupied many weeks.

David W. and Ron joined Eric in the immediate investigation of wasps, and when the others were reporting on their findings of a ramble to check on a nest of young pukekos these three reported briefly what most of us already knew: there was a wasp nest close to the school. They suggested that we try to track down the nest. We made our start in the room. We checked all the wasps that came into the room and saw that every one was a worker wasp. Most were caught; then the windows were opened again and a new stock of wasps made their short-lived visit. Again we checked and found them all to be workers. Then all the class had joined the investigation, and we broke up into small groups and studied the dead wasps and I was teaching for over half an hour. Drawings were made, and two children were preparing a slide of the wings for projection through the filmstrip projector.

Next day we tried them with several foods: apple, orange, honey, and some meat from Martha's sandwiches. We placed these in a row on a stump near the classroom and watched. Every quarter of an hour after the enthusiasm died down and we returned to other class work, two or three went out and checked the population of insects feeding. In every case they were eating the honey, although they showed interest in the apple.

9.00 a.m. No wasps, no bees, several ants were cleaning up the last of the honey we put out last night. We couldn't see any honey, though.

9.15 a.m. Fresh honey, no bees and no wasps yet, still a few ants. A car came up the drive and a man got out. He went into school.

9.30 a.m. Five wasps are eating honey. One bee was near it, or Lawrence thought it was a bee. The car is gone.

10.00 a.m. We saw fifteen wasps. Some came while we were there, and two flew away down towards the roadway. Eric squashed an ant.

10.30 a.m. We forgot to look.

11.00 a.m. Still lots of wasps. It was hard to count how many. Lawrence nearly got stung. Eric said they are all workers, but I don't think they are.

11.15 a.m. Ron found that Lawrence had been calling yellow Italian bees wasps, so there are some bees there too. Glennis said, 'They are Dad's bees, so don't squash them.' The wasps fight the bees sometimes.

Next day the honey feeding-ground was shifted, and no bees saw it all day and only a few wasps were seen. The watch went on. Wasps continued to come into the room, and little offerings of honey or jam sandwiches were placed in the sun for them. Necia said she saw one catch a fly. Derek said one had a spider. That may have been so, but more likely he saw one carrying off one of the small pieces of meat that Lewi had cut up just to see how big a weight they could carry away to their nest. We found out that both bees and wasps prefer honey to all foods, but that bees will not eat jam, apple, pear and meat, although wasps will.

I gave regular lessons on the wasps and used the

microscope for detailed examination. As well we discussed the value or not of wasps in the community. I was able to show specimens of tropical wasps and give life histories of the different classes of wasps, hornets, and related forms.

I saw that wasps came into the classroom more often on some days than others so I gave the children a problem: when do the wasps come into the classroom most? This led us to count the wasp 'population' every quarter hour through the day, and we kept up the observations for two days. We found that stray wasps came in the mornings, but that most came in the afternoons. There were most on the first day in the 12.45 p.m. to 1 p.m. period, but the next day there were very few then. Few wasps ever appeared before ten o'clock. I led the children to see that we would have to solve the problem in another way. I asked a second question: does the number of wasps have anything to do with the brightness or dullness of the sun? The next day was wet, and only two wasps were seen, during a brighter patch in the middle of the day, but the following day they came when the sun was out and especially in the afternoon. We made a rough scale of brightness: 1 for full sun, ¾ for mainly sunny, ½ for half cloud, and ¼ for mainly cloudy, 0 for all cloud and no sun. We related this standard to the balsa models we had made, but without much effect.

A certain amount of writing had resulted from fairly close associations with the wasps so far.

THE QUICK FLYERS

'I shiver like a cold baby bird. I think to myself I better run. All around me I hear nothing but a mass of wasps buzzing like revving engines. Awch! Awch!'
                                                        DEREK

STRIPED WASPS

'The flying wasps with bone stings which squirt poison when I squash them. And they sting the thing I squash them with and they die with their sting out.'
                                                        CLIFTON

WASPS

'This morning when I was getting breakfast, the wasps came inside so I killed them with a bottle. They were flying around my head making their noises, getting into the jam jars and sucking up the jam, and then having another go. Soon they went away from there and went into the cupboard with the bottled fruit. They are clever knowing where the fruit is especially away up high. They must smell sweet things.'
                                                        ROSALIE

The learning and observation provided topics for further writing on wasps, but in the beginning most writing was from past experience, often from observations even of years ago. At this stage of the development of the lessons I saw that I had to give content-lessons, and as well I had to involve the children with observations that required further statistical work which gave point

159

Wasp and marigold by Mary M.

to the lessons and allowed them to find out things that had scientific meaning. We studied ichneumon flies, horn-tailed wasps, the yellow wasp, Tasmanian wasps, and the Sirex wasp that damages pine trees. My contribution was as full as I could make it. I did not expect any part of my stories to be learnt, nor did I wish that any part of the work I had given them should be written up or used in accounts or reports. A great deal of work came out of these lessons of mine, however, such discussions as the one on the value or otherwise of wasps.

'My father says the wasps are good chaps; he's having no trouble with blowflies with the sheep now. He reckons the wasps eat the flies.'

'What a job,' said someone.

Allan told his story of finding a wasp nest on their coast farm and how there were no sheep blown on that farm at all. I was interested to see the interrelation of ideas such as this becoming part of our work. I found it scientific and meaningful.

I began telling stories, usually made up, about the various kinds of wasps in other countries: one story was about a parasitic helpful member, another about a pest wasp, and another about a solitary native wasp. I told a story of a family who had a large nest on their bush property and how they had to get help to destroy it because it was too near their bees. It proved to be the biggest nest ever discovered in the world, or so it was claimed. It was fifty feet long and grew from the base to nearly half way up a large rata tree. I felt that I was contributing with stories in the same way as the children did.

The stories and the wasps around us made us all very sensitive to their presence, and now and then someone would jump off his seat and flail the air. Mary screamed

Wasp nest by Irene M.

when one alighted on her arm, and Dennis held one by the wings, 'Look, I know how to hold them . . . Yeow!' He was stung. We used these experiences to show in movement the fear of an insect that stings. First we watched them flying around the room and studied their habits, and then we concentrated on wasps. Usually the children had their eyes shut as they thought of wasps, and slowly they began to mime a wasp.

Ron and Eric made their plans to find the nest. From our observations of wasps we knew that they regularly go to drink water. On this particular day the children went to the gully nearby and watched at a water hole as the wasps came, drank, and left. In each case the insects went away in one direction, up the hill. We went up the stream bed to another water hole and watched again, but wasps seemed to be going in all directions. Then we went to another stream a little way off and saw that the wasps were going away in the opposite direction, and therefore we assumed that the nest was somewhere between the first hole and the stream. We followed the wasps up the hill and sat down and watched the sky to see the line of flight. The number of wasps increased until we heard the low buzz of the nest in a nearby dry gully bank. 'The ground seemed to throb with the drone below the ground,' Eric said, when he told us the story of the discovery. We all went up and found the nest without trouble. Soon children were too close, and David was stung three times.

'Those are the guards, those ones. All the ones that

fly close around the hole are there on duty . . . That's why he "got" me,' he said.

'I want to see how many entrances there are; there were five on the coast nest . . . one, two, three, four, five . . . Wow! This is some nest, six, seven. Seven holes, one big one.' This was about all we or anyone else could find out about that nest. Reports were made on this discovery and in the diary and in personal writings.

WASPS' NESTS

'On the last day of the month Ron and I found the wasp nest, but first of all we had to see if we could find some trickling water. It's on Albert's place.

'We saw some trickling water and we saw some wasps drinking and they took off and I followed them up the hill. I left Ronny behind and he wondered what I was doing. I kept on running up the hill and then all I could see was a dot going along like a little car at high speed. I waited and followed other wasps and at last I saw a lot of wasps going into a hole. Then Ronny was behind me and we went to the hole but all we saw was wasps drinking. This wasn't it. I turned around and there were wasps by the millions going in and out of a little hole about two inches long and wide. That was great.

'Ronny and I said that we could find it. We went down to some water and there were some wasps. I think I could see their little tongues out. I know he was drinking anyway. He started to fly up the hill so I ran after him, I ran into more wasps but they were only flying to

162

get water. I said to Ronny, "This is not the nest." I looked around and saw thousands of wasps going into a hole.'

DAVID W., 12 years

Irene did a lino cut, as did many after this, and she wrote a short poem.

WASPS

Closer and closer up through the gorse
The buzzing noise came quietly nearer me
Nearer, nearer, closer, closer.
They swerved around me
Up towards the thundering nest . . .

IRENE, 13 years

DIARY OF THE WASPS

June 5th

'Today on the fifth of June, Valerie, Necia, Kenneth and David went with Allan and I up to the nest. There were less wasps than last time. They have bored right up from under and have come out the top. David got a stick and tried to dig them out but it broke. We had a look around and one wasp was on the ground and David killed it. It was fairly big and I thought it was a queen; it was skinny and long.

'They were flying over the hill and down to water. I had a look at a pine tree and there were a lot gathering gummy sap. The pine tree was covered with them.'

GRANT

163

Wasp by Allan

June 6th

'After school many of us went up there with a spade. David dug a hole down to where the grubs are and he picked up some cells and ran down beside the gorse bush. We all ran down and as he lifted up a piece we saw a queen wasp buzzing along. On that same day he was stung on the leg and the wasp was running up his pants and suddenly I saw him rubbing his seat.'

CHRISTOPHER

June 11th

'There were only a few wasps and we saw some getting dew from the grass. Mostly they were around the nest.'

ALLAN

June 13th

'We went up at lunch time and we hadn't been digging long before David I. got stung. We dug out the nest and the rest of the earth. The wasps came swarming out and we had to wait for them to settle before we could dig any more. We went up on Friday after school and really got to work. David W. dug a lot of the nest out and Owen came up to see what we were doing. We discovered a lot of cells with their tops on.'

BRETT

June 16th

'We have just been up there. The hole is six feet deep and five wide and there are chunks and layers of nest all over the paddock just where the boys left it. Barbara picked up one chunk of paper about six inches high and each layer was held up with props. She put her finger over one of the cells and wow, she was stung, but she was still game enough to carry the cell material home. Mavis dug up some of the paper cells and Barbara carried them because she has a cold and couldn't smell the stink.'

VALERIE

June 24th

'The nest is dead. We saw a queen wasp and a drone. The nest is well dead because of the rain.'

LEWI

The nest collapsed with the weight of children up the hill above it and this led to the end of the nest, but it took time. Several other nests were discovered in the valley by the use of the tracking knowledge. These were mapped. At this stage lino cutting and paintings were done by many. Wings were projected and ideas arose that were used in construction models. Mary's *Marigold and Wasps* was used as a cover for a special edition of the school magazine that was devoted to wasps.

Up to this point the study of the living insects had been somewhat remote. We had killed insects and dissected them, some had been mounted for the insect cabinet, and the study had been very much a pinned-out-on-a-board one. Allan's print illustrates this. Grant and others were some of the first to dig into the nest, and many brought pieces back to school for the study sessions that now began.

Full examination of the pupal stages was possible, and then the rains came and all that was left of the nest

Examination of the nest

settled into the mud and was later swirled down the hill. For a while we searched for queen wasps in heaps of wood and under logs, and then interest flagged completely. The study was over.

*   *   *

Some time after the wasp investigation was over, and just before the winter set in, we found that reports of the various herds of cows in the valley all mentioned that caterpillars were eating the pasture. Some herds had been turned out to winter pasture because of the shortage of feed. Some children went on excursions to interview farmers and bring a report back to the class to see why this year's milking had stopped so soon. One farmer and his eldest son came to the school with some of the evidence in a jar. Caterpillars by the millions were eating everything that was green in the paddock, and many pastures had been reduced to dry uneatable grass, and this was the reason why so many herds had been moved and milking had ceased.

We went to see a farmer spraying a paddock with a poison. He sprayed right around the infestation and left them to die out within it.

Some fifty caterpillars were collected and made up into a 'home' in a terrarium at school. Here they were watered each morning with 'dew' to simulate real conditions. Once a week the nearby infestation was inspected and we tried to see if the number of caterpillars and chrysalises had increased or not. At the same time we observed the habits of the fifty caterpillars in the terrarium. They became less and less obvious in the field and in the case in the classroom.

Again work was going on at home and in the children's own time. Eric, Jenny and Necia observed army worms crawling on the cows' legs and pigs' backs and assumed that they were carried from place to place in this way. Stuck on to the grass were white eggs which they thought were the eggs of this moth. We kept them and out hatched grasshoppers. We saw a great number of ichneumon flies about this time, and again and again someone observed a fly eating or possibly laying eggs in one.

Week by week records were kept until the caterpillars disappeared, but they never quite did. We then pulled the terrarium to pieces and collected the chrysalises. Only nine were found. We discussed the reasons for this.

'We could have hurt some so that they died.'

'Remember the poem Ron wrote about the slime that they spat out?'

THOUGHTS

Slimy, greasy feeling
Just like the slime of an eel
As some stinking army worms rot their bodies
Along the palm of my hand.
His divided body separates as he crawls along
I think to myself, why does the little beggar squirt
That slimy stuff out?
I suppose it is a protection against my wide hand.

RON, 13 years

166

Other suggestions were:

'The wasps were still around them. They could have been taking some.'

'Some might have died because this terrarium was not just like home.'

'But we fed them,' said Grant.

'It wouldn't take long for them to die if they got too dry or there wasn't enough food. I think there are a lot of chrysalises, really.'

The nine chrysalises eventually hatched into eight moths. These moths were divisible into two different kinds, which substantiated our belief in that there was really a difference in the caterpillars. The moths were inconspicuous insects and soon died.

'Sixteen per cent raised to moths, not bad at all,' said Ron. The children saw that if these percentages applied to caterpillars in the wild state we would surely have a plague.

*   *   *

In each case of simple environmental study, a number of side issues had come in and taken over the interest: wasps were found hibernating in the infested paddock, ichneumon flies were seen eating caterpillars, Sirex wasps were found on pine trees. Side issues appeared to be as valuable as the study itself. We were carried off in our observations when we found the grasshopper eggs.

A cricket trap we had made had little point (except that we caught the insects at successive instar stages) until we started to take counts each night. We found as I suspected that the population diminishes as the insects mature. We then made a family tree of five female and three male white mice, and the subsequent breeding added point to the study. Recording air, shade, and water temperatures in a graph showed us that water temperature altered slowly and little, whereas shade temperature varied somewhat more and sun temperature varied a lot. The children learnt that it was usually worth while getting into the water because it was not much different from the preceding day even though the day was duller.

I saw that at times there was a definite advantage in studying the unusual before the usual, the aberration before the normal, and the rarer example before the common one. When we saw a rare white heron in the harbour region we visited it and watched for a time. We studied white herons and egrets, and this led on to the study of the reef heron, which was common here. This approach allowed for more comparative work and more scientific discovery by the child.

In this way we made a study of the rare bush snail which was found on one of the three dominating hills of the valley, and then I laid down a pattern of working for the classes when they studied the common snail, *Helix aspersa*. As part of this work, the growth lines of snails were studied. Some children thought that they indicated age, but others suggested that they really could be only stages of growth. The important thing was that the animals were being studied and we were avoiding accepting knowledge without some direct observation.

When the common snail was studied next a large amount of work was possible in which the children could work more or less creatively. The scientific method of pottery work of some years ago (Chapter 2) was much the same as that which allowed them to solve their problems here. I saw too that it was closely related to the manner of solving design and craft problems. The experience in the first place in greater depth sustained the interest and made the expression possible and gave a pattern for investigation for others to follow. I liked the way that children were able to bring forward their own thoughts in this work; it seemed that facts were being used in the right way when they did that. The facts alone do not give the child the power of deduction, nor do they necessarily make him aware of that power. If the situation poses a problem, children are more able to deduce facts, the solution or both. Further we saw that study is of value only as it affects the children's thinking and imagination.

Unless the interest had been deep, unless the subject had been followed in fullness, and unless there had been a certain amount of the thrill of achievement through making advances on the basis of certain criteria, the impression, and hence the creative expression, is unlikely to be good. Nor will the process be of interest to them. Now and then certain writings and craft experiences led to such work as Valerie's *Caterpillar* or Jennifer's *Spider*.

SPIDER

Cold snuggle.
Not a sound.
Cold struck its woven webbed bed
Which curled round and round.

Cold struck its cornered bed.
Night covered in darkness
Black.
Buzzing insects struck its webbed bed.

But too cold for the helpless spider
He sat there
Not a move.
Thin sticked legs were shut away.

Raindrops fell
The night grew colder.

JENNIFER

LOOPING CATERPILLAR

I watched closely
An atom of life—
A little looping caterpillar
Crawling up my arm
Upside down.
He stretched then curled into a ball.
I touched him and he stiffened like a branch
Then continued his journey to nowhere.

Spider by Ken

His little nippers in front wriggle
For nothing . . .

VALERIE

RAIN DROP

Like a piece of glass
The rain drop shimmered
Shining with hidden light.
It made a small sun shine up
From the petals which held it.

MAVIS

Other lino cuts included an intentional error in the anatomy of the 'spider'. Kenneth said he thought it would look better that way.

*   *   *

In each case of the studies mentioned the introduction of number was of definite value for it gave meaning to a great part of the study. The study ceased being vague and rested on less supposition than usual, even though our scientific method may not have been very accurate. I began to use number in such things as English teaching, where we were concerned with usage in the study of letters.

Eric looked amongst his stamp collection envelopes as I was teaching a simple layout for addresses, letter-heads, and envelopes, and I was quick to anticipate him when I saw that he had selected a typed address in the style generally used by typists.

'That's all right for typing Eric,' I said, 'but not for writing.' I had to explain the observation to the others and was surprised to hear Eric's quiet aside, 'It wasn't that I was thinking about really. It was the full stop after Mr that I was thinking is wrong.'

I wrote a copy of his letter, and we found three other errors, assuming that my lesson was essentially correct. Because of this, after discussing errors and their significance in terms of understanding, we decided to collect a hundred envelopes and letter-heads of all sorts so that we could see how frequent errors are in the business world and in private correspondence. A hundred made it easy for us to use percentages, and I explained that since we really wanted to get a true idea of how often errors were made we could accept only the first hundred that came in—otherwise Eric might look for wrong ones and leave the good ones at home.

The envelopes came in a rush, and as they were collected each day they were numbered, until after three days the hundred was reached. They were a mixed lot: duplicated circulars were plentiful, mainly with personal envelopes, envelopes with advertising, official-looking ones, and one or two from business firms. We saw at once that some paper was better than others, that different typewriters had different type, that Mary's aunt wrote beautifully, and that one firm had used Health Stamps for a long time. We tried to find out which firms had their envelopes typed and we saw that solicitors, doctors, dentists, and all the big firms did; the grocer used his pen. These observations were interesting in themselves, and for the first half hour we quite forgot the original reason for collecting and numbering them.

'Number 57 is a crook one,' said someone.

'Can't spell our town.'

'Brown and Tilers always type their letters I see.'

'Here's Miss with a full stop,' said Valerie.

And so we began.

We formed groups so that everyone had four envelopes or so to look at, and on this basis the lesson continued. As errors were recognised we discussed them until, after we had been through a great many, I saw that we had to have some order or nothing of much value would result. I posed the problem: what should we do with them so we could find out more? Answers came in after ten minutes or so:

'We think we should mark them.'

'Our group wants to return the marked envelopes to the writers.'

'We didn't know what to do with them.'

'Go on, Mavis, I said we could sort them out,' said Eric.

'That's what we thought. We could put all the business letters in one heap and private ones in another and see who's cleverest,' said Waitemata.

That is what we did. We marked them first (so the first group gave us something) and then we grouped them into two groups. We counted and checked each heap after marking and found that we had:

| Business envelopes and circulars | - | 47 |
| Private envelopes | - | - | - | - | 53 |

Again we examined the envelopes and sorted out the correct ones in each group.

| Correct business envelopes | 17 out of 47 |
| Correct private envelopes | 10 out of 53 |

We saw that over a quarter of all envelopes we collected were correct The other percentages were worked out and the business people won, but not by much. We then discussed the probable reasons and again we collected reports.

'They have all the clever people working for them, and so they have to be careful, like we do at school here,' said Martha's group rather cynically.

When the laughter died down Mavis added her reason. 'We think that people who write private letters aren't worried about commas and full stops so much, and that is the reason why the business people won.'

'That doesn't explain why some people put a full stop after Mr,' said Brett. 'Surely it's easier to leave it out.'

'I leave 'em all out,' I heard Sonny say. Perhaps he's got something there, too!

At last we found several perfect envelopes for examination. We made a table of errors and found:

	Business	Private	Total
Full-stops missing - -	15	39	54
Incorrect full-stops - -	6	13	19
Setting out incorrect -	9	13	22
Spelling errors - -	3	0	3
Commas missing - -	2	29	31
Abbreviation full-stop errors	5	23	28
Other errors not listed -	1	4	5
	41	121	162

We analyzed the facts, and in this I saw that numbers disguised the truth from some of the children. But then Standard 3 had been so insistent on coming in with us that we had yielded to persuasion, and some grading-off of understanding was to be expected. Eric seemed keen enough and he was in Standard 3. I listed the statements and we discussed them.

1. Business people are better 'at it' than private people.
2. Private writers don't care about punctuation.
3. Business people make the mistakes about spelling our town.
4. The typists at the Te Puuru Dairy Co. are perfect.
5. Brett's aunt is perfect.
6. Nearly all private envelopes have errors.
7. Circulars are worst.
8. Full-stops and commas are common errors.
9. Some people put full-stops in for abbreviations when there is the last letter in the shortened form.

We checked all our information in the Oxford dictionary and other books of common English usage and I felt that we had come as near to real understanding of envelopes and what they mean as we could. We considered the importance of the errors, and decided that in the main they didn't matter much if we could read the addresses clearly. I found that I had been automatically perpetrating a simple punctuation error probably because of faulty observation or drill in my own schooling.

David went to the Te Puuru Dairy Co. and had a look at the perfect typists, who don't make mistakes.

'They're all ladies,' he said, and I could quite see that they were.

12

MATHEMATICS

I WAS constantly impressed by the fact that the children understood number more readily when they were doing some active problem with practical materials. I saw that our way of establishing scientific methods of working with clay gave real meaning to that study. In the same way the study of the river was assisted by measuring temperature in relation to our assessment of the amount of sunlight. I realized that I could teach a great deal of practical arithmetic and scientific method during the day-to-day studies in pottery work, nature study, and geography.

It appeared that arithmetic could be divided into two aspects: formal or, as I preferred to call it at that time, pure number and on the other hand social or applied number. As the 'pure' number (the work was always related as nearly as possible to the concrete) progressed and work became increasingly difficult over the years, I noted a gradual falling off in ability until now and then I realized that a child was attempting to learn a particular type of sum by a rote method that allowed for very little real understanding. At other times I found myself teaching a particular type of sum as many as

seven times before most of the group understood and could use the principle intelligently. I came to feel that the pressure of so much material that has to be taught in school is one of the main factors contributing to lack of success at mathematics. It was because of my concern at so much failure that I decided to divide the arithmetic time into two periods: in one we would explore and come to enjoy solving practical problems in which the amount of number might well be 'hidden' but just as real; in the other I would try to ensure that the situations had meaning and that everyone *succeeded*.

Firstly, I abandoned the long lists of examples that had to be worked through, and I spent more and more time teaching and discussing actual problems from the sets of examples. I introduced the idea that we could make up our own problems and found that this synthesis gave the person the understanding. We discussed problems rather more often than did them, and when the number was formal, for example if the problems happened to be subtraction of money, I asked again that the children should make up problems for themselves. I employed this same method when we came to work with practical materials. Children sought out their own 'difficulties' at all times and this gave added meaning to the work.

A beginning was made with clay at the time when we were looking for the best clay to stock the large bin we had made. Various clays were mixed to a homogenous state and rolled to a standard quarter of an inch thickness between spacers. From this a further standard eight-inch strip was cut. Each clay strip was marked with the name of the clay bed and the particular information relating to it. All were marked on one side into inches, halves, quarters, and, for one or two inches, even into eighths. We tested each other's strips and discussed our accuracy in marking. I taught parallax error and saw that everyone understood. I was pleased when children made up problems of this sort: if a potter was marking off a strip of clay and looking from the left of his ruler, making an error of an eighth of an inch each time, how much error would he have made in eight inches of measuring? Problem-making became a game. Our problem was to find a clay that had less shrinkage than the rest.

The strips were dried slowly and at the same time each day they were measured so that we could see if the rate of shrinkage was constant. Some strips cracked slightly and others warped out of shape, and we wrote reports on these qualities. I introduced the idea of percentage shrinkage, and showed what this meant in terms of ten or so strips. The children could work out the simpler ones, and I showed how each of the shrinkages came out. Other children had weighed out a two-pound block and found that it lost weight slowly over three weeks and then didn't lose any more.

Because the number work was linked with practical study, principles were grasped quickly, and it appeared that where normally the time required to teach the use of percentages was long the application of these principles to various other quantities, such as the pound sterling and weight, took only a short time. I felt that understanding was far superior, and I saw that the amount of rote learning was very low and that the general ability was a different ability from the product of previous arithmetic. Understanding the practical use of percentages generally meant consideration of *every* other problem in the same manner, with a consequent saving of time.

The percentages were calculated on a decimal as well as a fraction basis: clay B3 had a shrinkage of 12.5 per cent; D2 one of 10.6 per cent. A2 contracted 10 per cent when fired. Firing did not appear to alter most however. Clays from different sites were next mixed in various proportions, and new problems of proportion were introduced. Again shrinkages were measured, and at the end of each study we had a discussion and made our judgements on the new basis. In this way we found that a deposit of clay very near the school was as good as we could find.

Some years later the investigations were carried out again when the old clay seam ran out and someone pushed a vintage car body into the hole. At the same time clay of a new type was needed for the stoneware kiln. The clay had to be a precise clay body. Twenty or so combinations were made, and each was made into a small pot and tested at 1300 degrees centigrade. A reasonable clay was worked out and a number of dust bins became the receptacles of the required materials for the body.

These exercises in the use of clay arose out of a specific need, but it seemed reasonable to go on from selecting a desirable clay to some consideration of what could be learnt from slowly changing materials. An area of 8 inches by 5 inches was made in a tile former, and this was marked into square inches and allowed to dry. Weavers raised the question of materials that shrink. A small woollen jacket was traced on to inch squared paper. The jacket was boiled, dried and ironed flat and again laid on to the tracing. The considerable loss was calculated, working to the nearest quarter of a square. Lengths of string, wool, cotton, and linen were also boiled and shrinkages found. In six weeks of work the text-books had been referred to only for a little of the formal side of the work. I felt that the problems using hundreds, thousands, and so on seemed a little remote.

The problem of an over-crowded school next arose. We wished to make a work shed in which to do certain crafts. After a long discussion we managed to decide exactly what we wanted the shed for and how many people it would have to hold and what benches, chairs, and tables we would need.

Firstly we measured every desk, table, chair that it would have to contain. Then we took specifications of the amount of space these occupied. It was necessary to measure every article of furniture and every person who used the room. The investigation was split among different groups. Some measured people, their height, the size of desk needed for them, and the height of the seat from the floor. Others measured the area of seating necessary for all, and area around the old desks. Another group measured the room and drew in colour a plan of the floor area. Windows were measured by the small children, and poles were used to measure the height of eaves in an enthusiasm to draw walls as well as floors. In a few days the information had been completely tabulated, and a meeting was held.

The problem of room to work was real and discussions on the many new activities of the room were held, during which it was realised that most space was demanded by wood carving, stick figure carving and modelling, clay work, the science and nature display and experiment table, and the new shop which sold school necessities. Many of these could be included somewhere else without reducing the feeling and convenience of the workshop classroom. Ropes were looped to the rafters in the darkened loft of the unboarded

The scale model workroom

ceiling and platforms were hoisted up above head height to carry looms, stick figure groups, and a large Polynesian canoe Neville was making, but the problems still remained.

To solve them a suggestion was made that the floor plan group take their two inch to the foot scale and construct colour blocks for desk units, passage units and

176

other colour units for the teacher's desk, primer tables, and so on. Again groups went about computing the size of things in scale and water colour blocks changed these squares into the correct colour code. Units were exchanged and checked and corrections were made to satisfaction.

Another meeting was held and the large yellow floor plan was laid out and the blue desk units were shuffled into many positions. The desk marked Allan and Leslie had to be with Alma and Pearl, and Owen's with Trevor and Neville and so the planning went on. Corridor strips were laid and cut in and about the groups of desks and tables in the room so that spacing was real and sensible. Senior groups went on working when others were writing projects on other things. Possibilities were drawn in smaller scale, and the advantages of a certain plan were recorded and kept on file. In this manner several plans were made and a set of recommendations listed. Sometimes there were hours of calculation, and at others a lot of discussion and reasoning in groups. Arithmetic seemed to lose its isolation most of the time, but almost daily it was necessary to go back over a set of calculations and indicate why this particular sum was done in this exact manner. The degree of success, though, was satisfactory, and the interest was high. The plan, with the various scale blocks in their respective colour codes, did not give sufficient idea of what thirty-five children would look like going about the sort of activity that this project involved, so next, scale model people were made by all the children from the measurements of height and shoulder width. The difficulties of this transfer were attacked in groups in which numbers of heights were transferred to scale until each child alone or with help, made a small model of himself. The enthusiastic made model clay bins, work tables, mats, and curtains when the next stage of the project was introduced.

The laying out of all the scale models of furniture and pupils on the plan of the room did make the confines of those four walls seem cramped, and on the basis of expanding the room by foot strips a better size was worked out.

Then the project of building another shed in which to work at some of our activities was mooted. The scale materials were made and soon discussion was on the way. Whether the shed could ever be built was another matter entirely. (A shed was built and later was destroyed by fire.) A model was planned in great detail and gradually the project became essentially the senior children's work. Each drew full plans. Every calculation possible was introduced, before the construction itself was undertaken. The scale-model soft pine timber was cut to plates, dwangs, braces, rafter, barge boards and so on. The glue-pot and tack-hammers were constantly in use as each side of the shed was made, the rafters cut into each other, the window frames stuck into place. Calculations of the quantities of timber used by each group were tallied against estimates previously made. Perhaps there wasn't quite as much chance of making large errors as there was in the individual homes built in later years by succeeding senior groups, but problems after good healthy mistakes arose daily.

The model shed was boarded up, battened, painted, and the miniature people and furnishings finally laid in place. This represented a big achievement by the children, and it was also a very absorbing piece of social arithmetic. Many sheds and houses have been made as part of social studies and arithmetic projects and in every case the amount of understanding has been very high.

Once a year a project on time, the sun, and latitude was attempted. Solar clocks were made, shadows recorded and measured from the lowest sun in the mid-day heavens. In this and in every study I carried the work on over a lengthy period so that all children had an opportunity to be involved. I found a system of apprentices a good idea in that it was the responsibility of a group of three to teach the new member to take accurate records of the shadow length or the length of a leaf in some nature science experiment. Then one of the three could leave the group.

Day by day experiments in measurement became the part of arithmetic that held the greatest fascination for the children, whether it was the hour by hour calculation of the power used by the small electric kiln or the weekly totalling of the pints of rain water collected. 'If the meter read 11178.6 one hour and 11179.8 at the end of the next hour, . . .' was the simple type of sum involved. Example:

At 17 minutes past ten on Monday morning, July 23rd I read the meter before putting the electric kiln on to point one. We intended to fire our last month's clay work. Before the switch went on I read 1116.18 units. On the hour we read the meter throughout the day, and when it was switched off on Tuesday at nine o'clock. The reading was then 1138.16. We worked out that the kiln used 21.98 units which cost us 1.6 pence per unit.

Brett and I worked out that it cost 2/11d. to fire the kiln. We think this is very cheap.

Time	Reading	Hourly difference	Units
10.17 a.m.	1116·18	—	—
11.17 a.m.	1116·48	0·3	0·3
12.17 p.m.	1116·77	0·29	0·59
1.17 p.m.	1117·09	0·32	0·91
2.17 p.m.	1117.41	0.32	1.23
3.17 p.m.	1117·73	0·32	1·55
9.00 a.m.	1138·16	20·43	21·98

I stressed the fact that this quantity represented a definite quantity of heat in the kiln. Problems such as the amount of sugar used by the family arose: in a day Dad takes four cups of tea and one of coffee, one teaspoon of sugar in each, so he took five teaspoons. These were heaped on the scales. Mother takes half a spoon in seven cups of tea and coffee and so on until each child could work out the amount of sugar used in beverages in his home. This kind of social problem was found intensely interesting to children. The problems were concrete and meaningful and they made the text-book examples seem unrealistic. The many problems in terms of time, weight, miles, millions, again and again caused problems in comprehension. I felt that the complexity of general work in number was one of the reasons (apart from the too rapid promotion from one class of work to another) for the general failure of so many children.

Map reading on the local four mile to the inch multicolour survey maps was introduced and became part of story writing about such things as mustering and fishing. Such stories were generally 'illustrated' with a map. As well some children drew pictures of the country on the way. Descriptive geography crept into the work.

In number work children planned fishing trips to particular depths in order to catch deep-water fish. Calipers were rocked out to the particular depth and the distance was measured. All required data were written down. Problems of current, wind, and error were introduced as the children continued making up their own problems. Some even listed the fish caught and computed the total weight of the catch.

Of all the social number work done the map experiences proved the most satisfying. The answers to problems appeared in the hour by hour reality of the growing line of the journey, and the boy who added his Cuisenaire blocks, 4 3/8 miles and 1½ miles, to get the distance covered at 1 p.m. was engaged on many number experiences of value. In addition map work of this nature provided the closest link with other forms of expression.

By using these methods I found that I did not have to stress drills and skills so much. In teaching spelling I found myself taking lessons on the growth of a word into 'families'. In arithmetic I saw that I was taking many lessons on the meaning of particular skills and tables. The problems we were working with seemed to impose a discipline of their own. However I could *not* at any time disregard the need to learn tables. There is a time when a child understands tables and should commit them to rote. After two years or so of using Cuisenaire spatial material we saw that many children knew a great number of tables. Then we encouraged the child to begin to learn them by rote.

Of all the work ever attempted in number we found that the social experience kind had the most meaning. We saw that complexity in text-book examples prevented children from succeeding, and also in many cases set up a reaction in the child, through his constant failure, so that he did not like arithmetic and failed in the future. I am sure that this attitude of enjoyment assisted many to succeed where they would have otherwise failed. I am sure that the children went through the school with a clearer idea of the meaning of number, although few went on to pass in mathematics at higher examination levels.

David W. painting

13

THREE CHILDREN

THIS chapter discusses the work of three children: Irene who is thirteen, Valerie who is ten and David W. who is eleven. Valerie's work sprang from need to express her reaction to her environment. This led others to examine similar interests, and links can be seen between her work and David's bird work and Irene's *Night* poems.

Many branches of the curriculum are touched on in this study. The important point that it makes about satisfaction and need for 'completion' is that it is necessary for children to reach points of intense personal satisfaction in the completed work. The child needs to go over, abandon, and repeat a statement until such time as he reaches this stage of satisfaction.

VALERIE

Valerie ran excitedly from the school along the half mile or so of dust that was the way home. She was happy, extremely so, for the day had been a very satisfying one for her. It began with a story which had been on her mind since that morning, and the half hour it took her to write it was almost as pleasing as the comments the other children made when it was read to them. This was not all, for twenty minutes had been given to her to stage it as a play, and the play had been great fun, especially the bit where the torches danced over the walls and then went out for a moment and she had to 'bang' the torch to get them to dance again. So you see the play was really a lot different from the story, perhaps even more fun than the story, for much of the play was a 'make-up'.

She avoided her brothers and sisters at home, for she knew that they would spoil her joys with ordinary things; so, clutching an orange, a disappointing green-looking one, she ran on up the broken hill behind her home to live out as long as possible the thrill of having done

181

something highly satisfying that day. Valerie's satisfactions were the intensely pleasurable ones of having created something for herself and of having found that her statements had value with her fellow pupils.

MY WALK

'I was begging Mum and in the end she said, "Oh, all right." So I grabbed Clifton's knife and ran . . .

'Then "Oink, oink, oink . . . oink," John's pigs were out. I kept on going and I got really tired out; then my legs were ready to run again, so I did.

'I was up to Nancy's cream stand and I looked at my orange and I picked a piece of rind off and and started off up the hill. When I got to the top of the hill the wind was blowing into my face so I wrapped my coat around me and kept on going . . . I finished my orange just as I got in the door.'

LAST NIGHT

'I woke in the black; all I could hear was the squeak from the kitchen sink and the rattle of a door somewhere in the house, but all was dark.

'I switched on my light, but it wouldn't go, so I silently took out the bulb and put it back and switched it on again and it went. I went to get a drink and as I slowly walked to the door I could see two balls of fire in the kitchen doorway; it was our Cat Tabby. I switched on the dining room light and chased out the cat. I had a drink and took the torch that was on the small table into bed. I hid it in the clothes on the table to make it warm, then put it in my bed and jumped in myself. I lay breathlessly. Soon I switched off the light and switched on the torch. I played for a while and then went to sleep.'

The following day she continued with her stories and transcribed *Last Night* and *My Walk* into her book of stories and poems. The play was repeated by request the next day, as are the more exciting dramas.

Out to the front came Valerie to read the already familiar story. She re-read it for two reasons. This was a chance for her to do some *true* reading, and it gave her an opportunity to work towards a very good rendition as a result of a certain amount of practice beforehand.

'I was away, when you did this first Valerie,' said Owen, 'and I would like to suggest that you have a few of us who will be the noises, and if you like I will be the director.'

Every play that is repeated is different, and this one promised to be very different. Such spontaneous contribution had become part of the work and this happening reminded me that I had to keep an open, receptive mind to feel child development and needs.

'That would be really good,' said Allan, 'and could I be the cat that you have to kick out, Val?'

'And what about the rats scatting over the ceiling? They would be good in this play,' said Ted who was to be one of the torches.

While Nell and Mavis went fast asleep for they were to be 'Valerie' in this development of the original story, Owen was warming up the 'noises'. Some people were clock-ticking noises, some squeaked like mice and made mouse claws-on-walls noises. They tried out various combinations and agreed to a few cues for some of the particular noises to be incorporated.

LAST NIGHT

'Nelly, you and Mavis can be me again and you are asleep.' The play had begun even though several did not know where they fitted in yet. Owen ended up with six noisy people under his direction. Ron, Allan, David I. and Clifton were to be the rats. Ted, Brett, Necia and Mary were to be the dancing torches. Jennifer and two others were to be the shadows. The shadows is a good part and I felt excited by the poetry of that part of the play alone. Yesterday Jennifer had been a delightful shadow and I wondered about the possibilities of a shadow dance after this play was over. I found it unfortunate that we couldn't record her lovely movements, so that we could re-live such satisfactions. Movement is a fragment for reflection only.

'Last night I woke just as the clock struck twelve,' said Valerie.

'Ding, dong, ding, dong . . .' came from Owen's group. 'And I could see ghostly shadows painted on the walls.'

The shadows had begun their 'dance of the long shadows' with strong arm movements and long strides about the room. The frightening movements changed to body actions, and they were so absorbing for a while that Valerie forgot to go on. I thought again of the possibility of using this episode for a dance by itself.

'Then I felt for my torch which was on the table beside me: I grabbed it and switched it on.' The shadows stiffened and shrank back to bundles by the desks and watched the bobbing, unsteady, but always alive movements of the torches as they ran about the 'walls' and on the 'ceilings' on the way to the kitchen, from where already the noises of the sink with the dripping tap and the mantle clock could be heard. Gradually they grew louder and louder as 'Valerie' felt her way along the passage. Owen was directing them well. We saw the dark. We saw the hand holding the torch showing us the way to the sink.

'Valerie' whispered to 'Valerie' on their way so as not to wake the sleeping house and they stopped now and then when they heard a snore or a 'rat scuttle'. They drank. The water was cold and chilled their teeth. The cat appeared from a chair and sat in the passage way and looked with big startled eyes at the 'Valeries'. He was 'kicked out'. Then back they went through the menacing dark shadows to bed again. The clock struck the half hour in the background and 'Valerie', cuddled down with her torch and soon was snoring modestly.

The class had made their choice for that day and Valerie had worked out her players and set the basis for the mime-drama by her story-reading and commentary that carried the story. This allowed her to work out most of the detail even to certain suggestions for Owen's noise group. The wind in the eaves, the distant dogs, the dripping tap and the drinking noises were some she mentioned.

The play began in front of the story teller and progressed to the point where several centres of attention could be recognised, but a common core of experience went on through the play. At times some children stopped and watched but then were carried into some part of the production. At the end of the play I commented briefly. 'A very lovely play. The movements were good everywhere, and some were excellent. The words were enjoyable.' All I had said was that the play was enjoyable, now I wanted the children to discuss the particular satisfactions. I had indicated that I recognised that certain things were better than others. It was then up to them to do the rest. I had found that practice such as this in assessing the value of work, was most important to the growth of expression.

Valerie had begun a new thought in our work, and many weeks were to go by before the whole memory of it was displaced by other types of work. Perhaps even the next day there would be another child who would write a story that would take us off on some similar experiences. There was a core of reality in Valerie's stories, which numbered as many as five on the same topics. These were her experiences which were the stimulative direction for other children, who saw that they too had thoughts not unlike hers, and since she had enjoyed her story on that subject they too saw many possibilities. Often these extensions by other children are most valuable, even more valuable than the thoughts that began the work. In this case Valerie's further statements were also very pleasing and I have noted that once a child starts on such a programme of expression (in which some success starts off others at similar work) the stimulative value of this success 'charges' future expression and all is good.

It is not necessary for the opening topic in a new form of work to be necessarily good, but it must have a certain something that goes beyond interest, that children are quick to recognise and exploit. I have noticed very often that this acceptance of a theme or form of work has a close link with the possibilities for use of drama and art and crafts.

From the core of reality we see the extensions which are Valerie's. Her drama work on her story, which is part fantasy, her painting which proved to be an experimental sketch for the lino block which followed, and the lists of words about night (later used and extended by others) all followed *naturally*. This is an important word, for there were several who did not follow this pattern of work. (They were not forced to.) Valerie was yet to enjoy the satisfactions of seeing much other work done on the same topics.

There were many points of completion, i.e. where a

subject had been worked to the stage of complete satisfaction to the children who were engaged in that branch of work. It was necessary all the time to encourage, take stock, and repeat again and again, to reach that point where the individual could rightly say, 'Now I am happy I have got there, I have said what I wanted to say.' What other deeply satisfying completion is left for that child still in the same topic of work? There is no end to it, but interests and stimulation from some other source will ensure that a change is made just when it is needed. The child does not get bored for there is always some other group or individual at work at some other stimulative exercise. The only error that can overtake a child is for the value of the work to become less satisfying. This is prevented to some extent by regular assessments with the children. The child does not run out of latent energy. There is always the energy to reach that point of intense satisfaction.

THE LIGHT

'Our light has a long flame which shines into the dark and makes it clear. Sometimes when the moths and flies fly into the flame it shakes like leaves blown in the wind.

KATHLEEN, 10 years

LAST NIGHT

'Last night when I was going down to the cow-shed there beside me I saw a tree and there the morepork was singing out "Kweek, kweek, kweek". I got scared when I looked at him with his big black eyes.

'I suddenly looked away and there was another one singing out "Morepork, morepork, morepork" away over at Bruce Farm. I looked back and there with a rush of wings right out, the morepork flew away. I still looked at him as he flew away to the other bird. After a while I felt sorry for chasing him away.'

MAVIS, 9 years

'Ordinary but rather interesting stories, aren't they?' was my feeling. This story was to change the line of expression about the same time that David W. was beginning work on roosters. So interest did not stop; it changed.

'Dark is awake in the paddocks,' said Mary.

'The three square eyes of the window look at me,' said Barbara.

'There on the far horizon, far, far away, the half-chopped moon showed itself,' said Owen.

'Brrrrrr . . .' said Brett.

DARK

Dark comes quickly,
Clouds getting darker.
All I can see
Just before dark
Is the white of the Hereford.

ROSALIE

185

Rosalie's poem was one of the first to be written after the 'picture' poetry experiments and like her other poem here, did much to extend the satisfactions and total quantity of expression. The quantity of expression was in some ways related to the quality, and the absorption was related to the satisfactions. This did not mean that an essay of seven pages necessarily represented a triumph which led to further expression. It might well put a stop to further work. But intense statements such as Rosalie's did add to the right sort of 'quantity' of the expression on the general theme and this led to further work.

COLD NIGHTS
Cold nights make me feel awful
Shivering cold breezes come right
Into my face.
Cold feet as I walk on the concrete.

ROSALIE

Martha was one of the many new people who came in at a later stage in the growth of the experiment and who were engaged in the press-mould processes. (See chapter 2.) She had great difficulty in writing her real and actual thoughts and impressions on a subject. I thought *Dark Night* to be an exceptional statement for her. I have often felt that peak ability such as this has something to do with the qualities of other expression done at the time in that Martha is stimulated in the accuracy of her imagination to this point of finer realiza-

tion. The story is not exceptional and could well be called average, except that Martha wrote it.

DARK NIGHT
'While we were going to Totara on Saturday in the darkness, we could only see the lights of the houses shining like car lights. When we went further we crossed the bridge and I looked in front and there were two lights coming towards us.

'When this car came past, I could feel the wind coming close to my face.'

MARTHA

LAST NIGHT
'Last night when all the lights were out and after the clock had struck twelve, I woke up. Little light came through the window.

'My jaws were sore, too sore to move my head, so without moving it I pushed my hand out and got my torch. I went into the kitchen and ran the hot tap for a while and the water became warm. I took a glass from the cupboard and had a drink. My jaws were not sore any more now.

'I went back to bed, but what was that? A shadow . . . ooch, I giggled to myself. Ha, it was only a shadow that my torch threw out. I climbed into bed. It was warm and soon I fell asleep.'

VALERIE

Valerie's last piece of work in the series was a short poem.

NIGHT

Swaying sadly outside my window
A lanky-limbed tree stands
Like spirits white.
The branches wave outside my window
In the dark of the night.

Then swooping outside my window
A morepork claws
A branch of my tree.

VALERIE

NIGHT

As the night comes on

The clouds grow black
And the night goes black
Pitch black.

DAVID I., 7 years

NIGHT

As the day fades away the evening draws nigh
And seconds begin a new day
The hours pass by
And soon the arriving dawn
Startles the crowing cock.
The day half done when
Work's begun.

TED, 10 years

DAVID W.

David was walking carefully amongst his father's roosters and hens watching them, 'For we have to be careful, don't we, when roosters are about?' 'Big combs and such floppy wattles, big spurs like spears.' These were the roosters that he saw. 'Yellow spurs like some other bird I am thinking about. Ah yes, the pukeko; he has legs like the rooster but different . . .' And so began David's rooster story.

BULLY ROOSTER

'I thought to myself one day, I'll write a story, I thought of our roosters and how they run one foot after the other and I thought of the old roosters that have spears on their legs and big red combs.

'I reckon these roosters have legs as big as pukeko's but his are different in colour. The rooster's are yellow and the puk's are brown. The pukeko's toes are much longer.

'When I was out there the other day there were two roosters fighting. You know they always have their hairs at the back of their heads. But all of a sudden this rooster flew at the other and that was the end of the fight . . .'

With this story David did a drawing of the two bully

Two bully roosters by David W., 11 years

roosters that boss all the others in the run. Two roosters contemplating large grains of wheat scattered about on the ground. He wrote a further story in which there were hens and young roosters which didn't have their tail feathers yet and couldn't crow properly.

FRIGHTENED BIRDS

'Yesterday when I went to feed the roosters and the hens I mixed the mash and the hens rushed to the gate and just as they started to make a noise I went "Shoo!" and they all ran away going, "Gooo, goo, goo, goo,

goo-lo-o." But I know why they go like that. It's just like us going "Ow" when we get a fright.

'When I finished mixing the mash I ran over to the separator and they always fly over after me. Soon as I got to the separator they ran and ate the mash. They started to make their noises, but soon a rooster went, "rttt-ttttt" because he couldn't crow.'

DAVID W.

THE HAWKS

'As the hawks glide side to side, their wings look raw, I don't know why . . . I know why, it's because he is high up in the air.

'I can see the two of their heads looking down at us with their beaks curved looking down to see if I'm going to shoot him.'

HAWK ON MY ROOSTER

'Not very long ago Bevin saw a hawk on my rooster and just as he went Shoooo, the hawk was going to wring its neck. Soon Bevin ran after the hawk and it flew up half flying with his cruel legs hanging down, but the rooster was saved and it walked back up the hill.'

David was very matter-of-fact in these stories, which came one after the other. He didn't value them very much, certainly far less than the occasional pot he was making then. 'As the hawks glide side to side their wings look raw; I don't know why . . . I know why.' Such statements seemed to be a working-out of thought for David. We encouraged him and said that we liked his way of saying things, and I felt that here he had the essence of poetry. His description in terms of colour would not have been entirely new. He did not want to read over his story first and portray it as he had written it yesterday, but there was material in the story that he would use.

The play when it began was about moreporks and roosters. The girls did not mind being old hens. Ted was always a bird in these plays, because we enjoyed him so much as a bird. He was one of the two moreporks that swooped low over the hens and the two roosters just on dusk, when it was still easy to see that the night birds would have liked to tackle a small bird if they could find one.

After the play David said he wondered if the ruru (morepork) was really after the hens, for he had never seen them take one. 'Maybe they were after the mice and the dirty rats.'

David was rather forgetful, and usually preferred this sort of work where he could go on and did not have to look back. His ideas were ever pushing him on, away on to new expression, and when he was asked to repeat a play it was obvious that he was not very good at remembering. His spelling was a bit of an ordeal that day, for he needed constant help with all the new 'fowl' words and we made up a long list for all those who followed David's topic.

Roosters by David W.

A few days later, when he was writing to his friend in London, he was telling more about them. 'I am a lazy boy because I don't milk the cows; all I can do is feed the hens and get the eggs for Mum. We have nine chickens and they are all roosters.'

The next morning David came with a large piece of lino, asking if he could do a lino block of the big roosters for his craft work that week. This fine block was printed as a front cover for the current magazine and on cloth to make a large table cloth. The impact of this block was immense, for it was by far the best block that had been done up till then. There was, of course, a definite relationship between the one expression and the other, in that the satisfactions of the first led the craftsman on to make a further statement that is an enlarged and more developed expression. This was followed later by oil painting, and some years later he painted a large mural in oils which excelled all this. Similar developments of the one topic of expression have already been described in the work involving crabs. The same principle is found in the examples of fantasy called *The Three Hills* in the same chapter.

Among the many stories and poems Owen's two were in some ways the most forceful.

WILD SPURS
My rooster comes to me
On big eagle's feet
And goes away

190

On little horse's spurs,
Guarding and watching
The strutting hens
That tear the ground
And get the worms.

OWEN, 12 years

NGA HEIHEI

The rooster on twice five gigantic claws
Gets up on to the post ostentatiously
And sings his morning song
To the waking waves.

OWEN

THE ROOSTERS AND THE HENS

'One day long ago on a Sunday night I went down to the Hihi and on the way back a big old rooster came for me and I picked up a stick and hit him on the legs. It went wobbly for a while, but it got over it. It went up to the house crowing and I thought to myself, he is crowing to tell all the other hens and roosters to keep away from me. Then when I went to get the eggs he came for me again. I just said, "I'll get my stick and you won't have any more legs. So you better get out, out, out, OUT." '

MAVIS, 10 years

IRENE

Long before the work on roosters and other associated birds was completed, Irene was about to begin a new topic.

She thought for a while. 'No, today there is nothing that interests me. It is a dull· day, there is nothing to think about, I am lost for thoughts.' She went for a walk to rest for a while (the occupation that developed later into the nature observation). Perhaps she would think of something while she walked. 'Night, night, they all have been writing of night. What did I write about nights?' She looked through her story and poem book and came across *Night Time*.

NIGHT TIME

The sun goes over the hill
Night comes slowly, darker, darker
All is dark. Cats fighting out in the dark
Rats in the walls squeak, fight
Running about on the floor.
The night is dark.

IRENE

It wasn't thought to be much of a poem by the others but here and now it made her think again of the pukekos at home at night time. They were so noisy.

191

PUKEKOS

'At night when I am in bed, I can hear the wide mouths of the pukekos crying out. I listen again and I can hear more pukekos crying out in the dark night. Their words fade away when the wind comes slowly, slowly.

'The long legs of the pukekos are just like raupo stalks* standing up in the night breezes, but when I am just off to sleep, I hear nothing but the south winds . . .'

IRENE

This was the time when she was engaged in thought writing, the time when she experimented.

This was the thing she and others called 'thoughts'.

'I hear the morepork's voice echoing through the dark bush at night. His voice fades away like singing peoples.'

'Mist flows through the gullies like water flowing through the creek.'

'Slushy, slushy,
Slushy mud, damp tracks,
Cows make their bog noises in the mud.'

'Night, night comes slowly showing its dark
colour—black.
I hear the morepork again crying out into the dark.
He sleeps in the dark corner of the bush
And flies with heavy wings, then stops
And out again into the dark.
Dust flying into the air.

*Bullrushes.

It floats slowly past the iron shed and then it lifts
more dust up
And all are going together.

I hear the water streams flowing down . . .
The morepork has lost his note and has gone to
sleep.'

The rhythm of her words is sensitive. Her use of repetition, a rest, a stop, and again a change of thought, assists her feeling.

Irene did not want to write about roosters, but the 'dark' idea suited her. She knew a lot about birds of the night; the night work led on to this. The others were studying birds, too. We went to see goldfinches and yellow-hammers eating dandelion seed-heads, and then Sarah found a yellow-hammer that had just been killed by a car. This trip and the dead bird were made into a lesson in which I taught as much fact as I could, for I felt then that the study would follow birds for a while. The children were moved in genuine sympathy on finding the dead bird.

The feeding place of these birds was visited daily, and our record was a series of sketches telling something that we saw the birds do.

I had contributed to the work of Valerie to a less extent, but I saw clearly that I *was* an active part of that particular set of expression. I had been active in my teaching in the work on roosters, but this study was taught more fully than most. However Irene was the agent for the continuation of the work.

YELLOW-HAMMER

Out by the old sheep track
That leads into the tea-tree,
The little bird lay dead,
Lying with his wings under him
His eyes closed up—how sad.
The poor litle bird is dead.
His legs stretched out stiffly
And his head lay lazily onto the rushes.
The colours in his body shone
As the half light peered through the teatree.
The light sparkled on the dead bird that lay
      on the ground.

IRENE

*   *   *

There was clearly a link throughout the three sets of work, by Valerie, David W., and Irene. If the link was not obvious in the first worker's expression it came in at a later stage as the others were involved.

I saw that I had to teach as much as I could when opportunities arose, and that this was a better kind of teaching than I had known when I was following through topic after topic. If I did not teach at such times, the work soon became poor and lifeless. There appeared to be some stimulative value in this 'depth study.' The children did not make direct use of these factual lessons for their expression. Indeed I would have thought that wrong. I saw that many of my lessons were given to groups of four or five and that demonstrations and picture displays were enough to gather in others for extension 'courses'. I saw that some of the best teaching of facts, if that was all we desired, was done by the children at such times as they were asked to tell their own knowledge and all that I had spoken of in the lessons. The series of developments taught me too that I must use the environment to the full and encourage individual expression rather than class. This meant more and more individual and small group observation excursions on changes observed in natural things. These discoveries lead me to the development of the 'discovery' method explained in the section on environmental studies. David I. was one of the first children to illustrate the sort of deduction that I valued.

'Last week we saw a heron. I said to Brett, "What sort of heron is that?" He said it was a white heron because there were a lot of trees around it and it looked blue and white. The blue would be the shade or shadows cast by the tree. We talked about it and looked at things under trees and then we both thought that it couldn't be a white heron after all even though Brett's idea was a sensible one. We found out that our blue and white heron could well have been a very rare type of blue heron.'

BITTERNS

'Last night Val and I were coming home from school and Val threw a stone into the swamp and a large bird flew out. Val called, "A bittern!" At that time Mum was coming to school so we told her. It flew up into the gully on Albert's. It had a blunt beak. We thought that it must look like that, so we would think it was a stump.'

NELL, 12 years

I saw that as the pattern of teaching and observation went on, there could be expression which went on without much action from me. Some work arose as a result of this child beginning in which I could become more and more involved, and then there were studies which I could instigate but which rarely resulted in very deep expression unless the children were allowed some opportunities to extend their thinking for themselves or work out their ideas through some activity such as drama or painting.

BITTERN

PLONK!
That was the stone that I threw
Into the water.
FLAWWWWWWW!
OW!

What was that?
A bittern?
Yes, that was a bittern.
I threw a stone on the water
And that was what got up.
And I jumped when I saw it—
That long, stick-long bittern.
Up into the gully;
Soar down the slope,
Now stopped and still as a stump.

VALERIE

It became more obvious that at times the work developed into small units of work. In this way David H. developed his interest in pheasants into a study of his own. This sort of splitting into many such interests usually took place at the end of a satisfactory study. I came to recognise the symptom. At such times I usually worked in some study that required a good deal of stimulative experience in dramatics, often in social studies. This started off new work.

14

THE PLACE OF VALUES
IN THE DEVELOPMENT OF CHILDREN

WHEN we began this creative work and for some time afterwards we did not recognise any particular result or aspect of it that was better than any other. The first recollection I have of the emergence of a sense of values was in the appreciation and then the use of clay itself as a material having certain definable qualities. I saw, and others too made the same observation, that clay could be *used* to the full value of its plastic and textural quality, and that there was a relationship between the satisfaction derived by the individual (and later the others of the group) and the value of the pot or figure made. From that point onward we were consciously engaged with values in education. At first this took the form of intuitive selection of pots and figures that gave satisfaction to the observers. Most children contributed towards the one standard of values. Later I realised that this was not necessarily a good thing, but this was after I saw that there were different standards of values developing among the children. For instance, David W.

became the authority in the school on the value and satisfactions to be derived from the pottery; Jennifer became one of the best painters, and Irene one of the better poets.

When these first judgements were made, certain pots were placed aside because we recognised that they were better than the others. Then I saw that the general mass of activity that I called *work* contained all manner of statements: clichés, superficial attempts that involved no real introspection, muddled expression, good things that had remained undeveloped. Rarely was there a piece of outstanding work. After three years, when examining a large collection of pottery done by Neville, I saw that his work contained brilliant pots that had gone unacclaimed before. It appeared therefore that creativity involved values, but if values go unrecognised among a mass of inferior work there is no growth. As soon as judgement begins, as in the selection of some better pots from the mass of work, the influences of the inferior are no longer felt so much, and there is a need and even

an urgency for the individual to order his thinking and working to and beyond the recently established level of experience.

Much of the teaching that I thought assisted expression was not effective because I did not at first know how to discriminate between good and bad work. I gave undue importance to the formal and factual side of the programme at which the child of higher intelligence 'succeeded'. At first the standard of judgement was always my own, and I see now that the work of the school reflected my inability to judge well. My measure of the relative success of each child placed the children of lower intelligence in a position of lower privilege and importance. Since some children could absorb information and skills well I had thought it reasonable to value this most. It was easy to place more importance on rote learning than on conscious understanding by the child.

Any progress that was made in the beginning arose out of my own recognition of the needs of the situation, but I saw that it was the children who should eventually be making such assessments and who should be becoming more proficient at knowing their own needs.

When the first pots were taken from the kiln and the children talked about them, I saw that most of them knew that three or four were better than the others. In the same way certain paintings, poems, stories, and lino prints were selected as better than the others.

I had a responsibility in these decisions in the same way as I had earlier, when no judgement was made of the value of work. The standard had really depended on me at that time, and in the same way I had to make a contact in spirit with the decisions that were now being made. I saw that it was desirable that children should, at some time in their growth, be able to progress in some manner of expression without contact with a teacher. Experience has shown me that individuals who do not reach this point, soon suffer the levelling-down influences that take effect as a result of the weaker statements taking place around them. This happens as soon as there is no discrimination between good and bad work. Soon the children appear to have little critical ability. So we discussed the work done each day, especially after an event such as the opening of a kiln or completion of a drama series, with a view to selecting the better aspects for examination. We tried to find out why one pot appeared to be better than the others, but generally we concluded that it just *was*. This led us to set aside a special place in the school where such things could be kept. As time went on, more and more space was given to the display of other sorts of materials and crafts in this 'shrine': coloured stones, leaves, branches, even well-shaped bottles were displayed there at times. I saw that it would be desirable that the shrine should be extended to embrace the whole school room, and eventually the whole school, if it was possible to reject the poorer things from the grounds. I have pointed out earlier how valuable this display became to the various creators, especially in times of 'stress' when the children felt the need of some realisation of success.

Gradually the room was 're-decorated' with children's work, which was displayed only if it was considered of sufficient value by the group or by certain individuals like David W., who we knew were better judges of art and craft values than the rest of us.

The value of this belief in the importance of the environment has been seen over and over again, as new pupils came into the school. Very soon these children were working at the same standard of things as those around them. While much of the work displayed in the rooms was of stimulative value, it was also decorative and imaginative. Mobiles allowed for imaginative thinking that the pencil-case and rubber didn't.

I was given reason to reflect on the habit of many craft and art specialists of selecting work from a classroom and taking the best away to show other children who have not begun to discriminate for themselves. By this action both classrooms are being hindered in their progress towards work of better value: the first room has no selected work of value by which to raise its standard, and the second cannot really be helped until the better examples are selected by the teacher and the children *from their own work*.

Following the development in pottery and other crafts, we began to select the better poems and stories for display with the visual work. For a time these were pinned on a special board. We found that an important part of the process of assessment of a painting, story, or poem, was to select the images, elements, or interesting aspects from the whole for separate recognition. A good deal of technical advancement took place as the result of the cutting out of 'good pieces' from otherwise uninspired paintings. This sometimes led on the painters concerned to further expressions of the same idea, but more generally it influenced what they had to say in later paintings. Sheets of small sayings often represented all of value that existed in the work. Minor statements and good ideas and, later, simple images of excellence had their place in the display of ideas.

Two papers from Nell, when she was eight, one about 'figgers and niggers and diggers' and one about the turkey gobbler were pinned up. Such work was to be read by everyone each day. Nell had two pieces there, Allan four, Eric one, and some had none. There were all sorts of reaction to this new board. Allan was happy to have some work on the board, and he became worried when he had nothing there. Some people who had nothing there showed no interest in what was displayed. Others became very pleased on the times that they did get a piece up. I maintained the rule that everyone had to read the work presented for I felt that we all had to be involved in these values. Everyone had to play some part in the judgement. This was easy enough, for all that I asked was that they should be able to select some good use of a word, phrase, or image from a piece of work.

Some of the children did not want Nell's *Turkey Gobbler* and her other poem to be removed to make way for new things. These and another one about sparrows had to remain. They were the first setters of standards.

FIGGERS AND NIGGERS

Figgers and niggers are just like diggers.
I like my Daddy because he likes niggers,
But he does not like diggers.
They have turned up shirts.
They have big pick axes.
They work in coal mines.
Out they come as black as soot.
Their wives are wild,
Because they have to wash their clothes
They don't come clean too easily, do they?

NELL, 8 years

THE TURKEY GOBBLER

'The turkey gobbler fluffs up his feathers, spreads his tail, swells his head ornaments, rattles his wing quills and struts and gobbles to let the people know that he is glad. She sometimes does it too, to tell him she has laid an egg.'

NELL

The need for a place to display these better statements had emerged. When the children refused to displace good work I saw that some sort of cultural magazine was needed. It was the same development that had made the children keep the pottery on the shelves. I introduced the idea that we could best preserve poems such as Nell's if we had a magazine, and also that every child could have a copy to keep at home. Some children felt that the magazine should have a particular form, but I hoped that it would just grow, then it would be most likely to serve our purposes more adequately. I saw that lino blocks could be included and perhaps even silk screen prints. I hoped that it would give new purpose to skills such as spelling, handwriting, language usage, and grammar. Children's jokes, riddles, and puzzles were handed in for the first edition, and after long consideration all were rejected as unsatisfactory material. In the same way, and for the same reason, the children rejected much poetry that adults write especially for children.

A work-routine was soon built up that allowed for writing, proof-reading, assessments by the writer, then by the group, and finally by the whole class, if it reached that level. The copies were then corrected by two groups of examiners, typed or written on to stencils, and printed. This activity was a fully permissive one in that we could use any idea or form that occurred to us for particular magazines. Thus every magazine was given a new name. Generally it was given a full-page lino-block cover. Some issues included pages of news and reports of one sort or another, but generally the magazine was about work that arose from class work and personal expression. Some of the names given for magazines were: *Too Right,*

199

Full Moon, Wild Spurs, Te Karaihe Roa, Puhia Te Wheri, Rangi Ika, Nga Manu Pai, Ghost Post, Crabs' Blab . . . Sixty or seventy were published over a period of seven years.

One of the first magazines, *Ghost Post*, named by Varley, was also illustrated by him, and the story was written especially for this edition. This was not usual that work was done specially for a magazine. In *Crabs' Blab* the front cover and the poetry *Lonely Loft* were part of Joyce's ordinary work. Michael's *Fantail* block was selected from his nature work. Barbara's *Cakes*, Owen's *Fantail*, Michael's *Morepork*, Anna's *Pied Shag* and the *Sailing Bird* were some of many bird poems and stories that were being done by children in the midst of an activity in bird watching. Magazines had now become an outlet for all aspects of class work.

GHOST. POST

THE ABBEY OF DON'T KAIR

'At the abbey and kirk of Don't Kair there were a lot of people (ghosts) who were dressed in short night shirts who were vanishing and appearing all the time. All this happened quite often in the flash of a second.

'At about the year 188 B.C., when they were building the kirk and the abbey, the slaves were nearly worked to death and when they died as they usually did event-ually, they were put inside, into a sixty foot hole (for the foundation) to hold up the hundred foot steeple. Ever since 129 A.D. those ghosts have haunted 129 miles North, South, East and West.

'One time a man called Joe Consant got a good eye-full (slang) of one who said he looked like Du Slagen (he came from around the basement). That was where he was put by his brother De Du Slagen (he lived at the top of the steeple). Both these ghosts came from near the French border. When Joe shot at De Du Slagen, he turned into flames and vanished. Another one appeared from above the door and breathed fire all over the place.

'There were meant to be walls all around the place and a manor house but the ghosts were that thick that the workmen could not turn round. They were as thick as old gourmets of York, so none would take on the contract. In the year 1100 A.D. the governor of York said that the ghosts would be killing the good priest Willingham and all his good men.

'Now the manor is all tumbled down and I am partly holding it up. The bell rings in the steeple at 11.59 p.m. every January the 33rd and the people say that when the building was finished all the ghosts appeared and disappeared eighty-one times.'

VARLEY

LONELY LOFT

Down in the blizzard's lair
Where the winds roar,
In tiny coves
All is desolate.

Old, old crabs,
Unpoked by boys
Wander the beach
Without the sound or noise.

Seagulls croon loftily
While out in the deep blue sea,
The dip, dip, dip of a fisherman's oars
Breaks into the stillness.

The flip, flap of the waves
Under the sun's red glare
Increase the eeriness
Which grows the more I watch.

Sheep climb the rocky hill
That form the background
Of a noiseless beach.

JOYCE, 10 years

FANTAILS

'Early on Saturday morning when the fog had rolled over the hills, we went into the bush. As I was walking through the tall kanuka trees I saw a gay little fantail come to us. It fluttered and fluttered around until it went straight to a ponga fern tree and there we followed it. Before we got there I saw two fantails stripping moss from a kanuka tree and suddenly I turned around and saw a gay headed little fantail fluttering towards the ponga with pieces of horse hair in his mouth. When it landed we knew straight away that it was going to make a nest.

MICHAEL, 12 years

CAKES

'When Mum bakes cakes I watch her, but then she gets mad at me and tells me to set the table so she can get rid of me for a while. If I am finished before her she tells me to go to play. The one thing I like is watching Mum bake cakes, I don't know why but I do . . .'

BARBARA, 8 years

FANTAIL

Down in the teatree
As the wind goes ooooo-ooooo
OO-OO-OOOOOOOOOOOOOOOOOOO-
Through the teatree and gorse,
The fantail echoes,
Until his pebble-big heart
Is going thump, thump (fast)
Then suddenly he goes after an ant
And puts his jaws around it.

OWEN, 9 years

MOREPORK

In ancient days there was a bird
Who flew near to the pa at night.
It is said, if you kill a kou kou,
You will be killed by his mana.

When you go into the forest you
Will be killed by his mana.

Late one night a tribe of Maoris
Went through the forest to attack the pa.

And the kou kou knew
They were going to attack the pa.

So the owl flew slowly through the kanuka trees
Until he reached the pa.

And there he perched and started to talk
On a rimu tree in the language of birds.

He told the pa the tribe was coming
To attack their pa.

And the Maoris in the pa heard the bird
And knew that they were going to be attacked.

MICHAEL

PIED SHAG

'On Sunday when I was on the beach I noticed a white object lying below the sand bank and I went over to have a look at it and I found that it was a dead pied shag. I picked it up by the beak and had a look at it and getting tired of holding it in this way I dropped it and kicked it right away onto the sand and then I noticed a silver ring on the right leg. I carried it to a safe place under a pohutukawa tree and I took the ring off and I saw printing on it and it said 18860 send to Dominion Museum, Wellington.'

ANNA, 13 years

THE SAILING BIRD

Heaving over the waves so high,
A white bird sails with battered wings
Then tired and weary it lands on the lonely
    beach
Called Motukahakaha.

203

While it battled for its life the cruel waves
Swept it high onto the beach
And there it lies with a ring on its right leg.

ANNA

The magazine was a success because it grew out of the normal work. The children did not write specially for the magazine. It was as fully integrated with school activities as possible. It was stimulating to the writers and to the lino block cutters. It was a record to which the children could go back for satisfactions. It embodied their increasing perception of values in expression, and it involved the craft of making a book out of little, and this in itself appealed to the children.

The magazine provided social and cultural satisfactions in the same manner as the 'shrine' had done earlier for the visual arts. When the days were short, dull, cold, and wet, the magazines were taken from the book shelves in many homes and the children read them again and again. Some people, like Nell, began to write again.

It is not enough to consider the value of a piece of work only when it has been completed. There are points of indecision during the work when children should apply their intuitive ability to judge. This is generally encouraged in an informal way, as the following example shows.

One day Varley was painting and it was going very well. I noted the general hum of activity about the room that added to the atmosphere of work. David W. was moving from person to person commenting on what he saw, when Varley came over to look at David's painting. Now David 'could *really* paint' and as Varley came over the floor, carefully stepping over the two or three who were sprawled out on mats, painting, I saw that he was looking anxiously at his friend's paper.

'Needs something down there—oops, sorry Brett—down there at the bottom. Why not leaves like those up there? I don't like your two figures. They're better than the ones in your last painting, David,' he said.

'Hmm, I don't know what to put in there. Some texture I'd say, but will it need to be dark or light like that there?'

I didn't expect that he would follow this advice exactly as he was told. 'It was good of him to get me going again,' thought David, 'and I don't help him much.'

David walked over to Eric and took him back for a talk about painting and story behind the *Three Hills* fantasy paintings that he was working at. Then he began to paint in the decisive manner that he had worked out for himself.

'Why no leaves?' asked Varley.

'Grass would have been better like I said,' added Eric.

'Pebbles. Pebbles are good textures and anyway it needs dark down here below. They are the lovely stones that we saw in the creek yesterday. Weren't they?' he added.

'I like it now,' said Derek, who either liked or disliked things.

I felt that this was a good way to be, for indecision usually meant that the thing being examined was not very good. At least this was true for work encountered in school. It could be disastrous at other times.

As the children's criticism and assessment developed I became content to hear such statements as these.

'I like your long story, but I was disappointed that you didn't say more about the things you people were talking about after lights out. You made me quite scared with your description of the trees about you as you came from the beach.'

* * *

'I'm not quite sure about this pot, Derek. I felt it was going well when I was making it but now that I look down on it from a different angle, I'm not so happy. What do you think about it?'

'I don't like it,' said Derek, but then we expected that from him.

'Oh, a bigger lip would fix it. Here, let's have a go!'

'Not on your life, this is my pot. Anyway I think I know now what I should do. I will build it higher and then a lip.'

* * *

'I think we should do the section on the launching of the canoes again. I think we should think about the size and weight of the canoe more and then the play will be better,' said Mary in a recent drama session.

* * *

'Moths about the window light
They tap at the pane
And swarm at the light.'

'I like that very much. I think Stuart knows a lot about moths. He writes as if he *is* a moth. We would know that the pane is a window, but the only thing the moth knows is "window light". Perhaps it doesn't even know it is a window.'

'You mean it only knows *light*,' said Jennifer who likes to have everything explained fully.

Jenny may be a teacher of quality one day. She always thinks things out completely and rounds off the half statements of others. That is why many take their literary problems to her.

On a Friday we selected Ronny's story for study. It had been read over that morning by a small group and a number of comments had been written below the copy by the group who examined it.

'We began on the steep section beyond Motunehunehu rock fall, where last year we missed so many sheep in the first muster. Even as I came around the lee of the hill, I knew that the morning's breeze was a blustering strong wind from out of the sea. I followed the sheep tracks behind the ever increasing mob and the wind-silent dogs and I was quite suddenly aware that I wasn't doing much to help, except perhaps by being there, but that did not occur to me even then. It was a moment's thought as if I was watching myself and had done all this before . . .'

The story went on, and though the end of it wasn't as good as the beginning the whole was the sort of thing we liked. He read on to the herding of over a thousand sheep at the pens on Whakapuku Flat, but he did not read the comments that the small group had written down. In the discussion time these questions would be put to the test.

Valerie opened the comments. ' "Wind-silent dogs" is beautiful. It makes me try and say something good, such as . . . er . . . river-wet cows . . . But that's not so good is it?'

'Wouldn't it be terrible to find out that someone had said that before and not Ronny?' added Derek.

'In 1588 on sighting the Armada for instance,' said John.

'I like your beginning Ron. It's just the best writing you ever did, but I think you went astray after a good beginning.'

'It's like David's story of yesterday about his motor bike bits. The way he said it, I mean,' said Mavis.

'Sort of flows,' said Dennis.

' "Rock fall" is a lot better than a lot of rocks.'

'I like the way you brought your thinking into it, Ronny,' said one of the older girls. 'You've made the story part more real because of that.'

'Now what did the group say? Oh yes, "wind-silent dogs". They liked that and the thinking part, and it's for the magazine. That's good Ron.'

'Whakapuku! What a lovely word!' said Valerie.

From fabric design by Barbara

15

VALLEY SOUNDS

ONE of the rarer opportunities in recent years was the set of circumstances that caused the writing of a full length narrative poem about our valley. As a preparation for the dramatization of a story, drama and movement work on the awakening of the valley was particularly satisfying on this day, and after this some of the children began writing a few thoughts in poetry. These were so interesting, and we liked them so much, that others set to work, and this led the children into recording the happenings in the valley. Soon they had planned out a record of the happenings of a day. At no point until it was completed, however, did we know quite how the story would go, for those who had pencilled in their preference to write about one particular thing ignored the line of the developed story of the previous writers.

This is the story.

VALLEY SOUNDS

When morning comes the stars wear away
And people see the shadows of the windows.
They think they are ghosts in the ghostly scrub
And they hear the morning rooster crow.
                                    DAVID I., 7 years

No human shape or sight of soul is seen;
All of the valley is silent and misty.
A cock crows under the dark blue sky,
Another crows and yet another.
                                    BRETT, 10 years

So early in the morning there's a thrush
Singing so cheerfully on the power line,
But about to fly into the wattles.
Now he's tired of singing and is eating.
                                    DAVID W., 11 years

The rooster crows when the dark blue world turns pale
And the hens jump off their pronged beds
And walk around the roosters' legs
And still the roosters crow on.
                                    BARBARA, 10 years

Farm at Oruaiti by Ken G.

Many hear the first song of the blight bird.
The waking people hear the wild cats fight,
While horses give their morning snorts
And cows their lazy morning yawns.

OWEN, 12 years

As the wind creeps over the hills
The little grass-heads shiver in the cold.
The muddy puddles are iced up,
And then a cock crows again in the valley.

CLIFTON, 8 years

The wind blows at the flowing tap,
It blows the branches of the blue gum trees.
Making the branches sway and loudly creak.
Then the hairs of the blue gum sway and blow.
Off they come and sweep the brown earth floor.

DAVID I.

Around the long meandering river
The shiny pukekos sound their fog horns.
The frost-bitten ferns lie around the banks.
The bitten ends sway in the frosted wind.

VALERIE, 10 years

They hear a rat rumbling around the wall
Trying to find his dirty, stinking nest,
And through the hole he peeps his head,
Looking around the room for food.

TED, 11 years

208

And from the red sky comes the grey-green duck,
Flicking his yellow beak to wake the pa.
With a stir the women wake first;
Out into the cold they step with a shiver.

TED

The people wake from their beds with tired eyes,
Listening to the wind blow past their houses.
The women get up and put their slippers on,
Shrinking, shrinking to get the cold clothes on.

IRENE, 13 years

Waiting around the sheds are the mooing cows,
Then people start to milk them,
With the puffing plants,
Making noises as they milk.

ALLAN, 12 years

As the cows clicketty on the concrete,
They stamp on the hardness, mooing to the calves.
The live rubbers go up and down till empty.
The live rubbers move, till her bag is dry.

DAVID W.

When women rise they shiver in the cold,
Then slowly they walk the bathroom passage.
The trickling and waiting for gushing waters,
While the patient women are in waiting.

NELL, 12 years

The blue heron stands in the early world.
Looking like a freezing blue cloud in the morning.
The dogs pull their chains along the ground
Around and around the house with the chain.

IRENE

Someone sees the cream truck come into the valley.
He stops. Bang, bang, clanketty, clank!
They hurry so they will be in time,
As he slowly comes along the frosted road.

BRETT

Galloping around the paddock is a calf
Blaring to its mother for a feed,
And as she feeds it she is bunted.
Then it is quiet and goes to sleep.

CLIFTON

When the boy goes to feed the lamb, it bites the tit.
When the lamb has finished it calls for more,
But the boy walks down the green grass floor
And the lonesome lamb baas and baas and baas.

CLIFTON

Pups skidding to get near their mother's tits
And squealing underneath the mother—a little pup.
The farmer calls for the mother dog.
'Here girl, here! Get away up there you mongrel!'

DAVID, 12 years

On a pine tree above the river,
A lone blackbird sings his warning to the other
    birds.
One and yet another thinks, 'Bossy!
I can do the same,' and so a fight begins.

BRETT

The golden gorse shines in the red shining sun
And the blue sky fades itself and grows dark.
Then darker it grows and the gorse does not shine
Its gold again.

DAVID I.

The peppered gorse grows on the grassy hills.
When the gorse gets wet the colour slowly changes,
The brown earth shows through the gorse and
    grasses.
The rain drips on till it makes small streams.

ROSALIE, 14 years

As the leaves on top of the oak tree drink,
The ones underneath get only the drops,
And the ferns underneath get none,
But the cruel claws of the frost nip at the top leaves.

VALERIE

The rain races around the dull hills.
The wind echoes throughout the sounding gullies.
The floods moan away down the river,
Rushing over bent under weeds.

IRENE

Water rushes down swiftly, making rings.
The sound in the gullies keeps on,
Loudening his noisy voice,
Then fading away as the waters die.

IRENE

The slashing waves shout upon the beaches
And soon comes the angry tempered thunder.
Suddenly the lightning flashes quickly
And animals run under damp trees.

MARY, 12 years

In the drain lives an ugly looking eel
With long slimy body,
Squirming around like a big water snake,
Chasing the little fishes around the pool.

CLIFTON, 8 years

Through the hole in the bridge dangles a bait,
Which the cunning old eel has not touched,
And in his hole he soundly sleeps unbothered,
While around the pool a single fish swims.

TED, 11 years

The bittern is a half-dead rotten stump,
Stump-still above the stump-still waters.
While the moon grows smaller and the sun brighter
He stands above the stump-still waters.

VALERIE

210

Fantails and mosquitoes by Michael H.

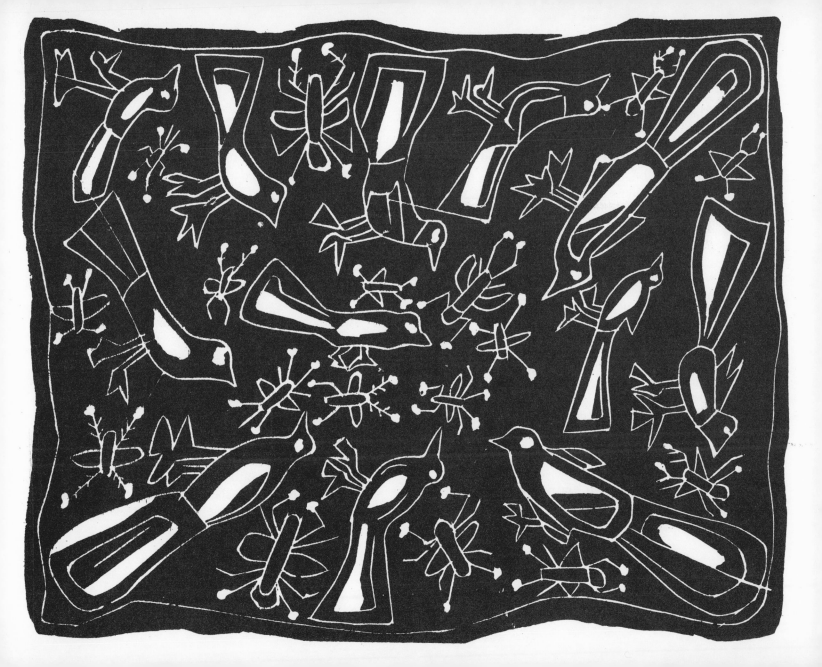

Flitting through the teatree comes a stranger.
A fantail flitting down to the shining water,
And lands with a flit, a branch beside his head.
Then with a jump the bittern flies away.

VALERIE

The gobbler with his golden spurs tries to show
them off,
But no one likes his golden spurs.
The turkey from his willow roost gobbles
To his grumbling wives and peeping chicks.

MAVIS, 10 years

'Yoo-hoo,' someone is calling her husband from
the fields.
The weary man trudges to his house.
'Roast beef for dinner,' says his wife.
Soon they settle down and start to eat.

BRETT

When they leave the house to get the sheep
The poor little pup jumps and yuks at the chain.
Suddenly the twisted chain breaks
And the eager little pup goes up the hill.

OWEN

Around and around the wiry stone tracks
The horses plod along to Pukemiro.
Over the four-feet logs and through boggy swamps,
They plod along the hills to the coast.

ALLAN

As they come in to the open they hear the first blare
Of a wandering calf.
As they ride down to the cabbage tree,
There is the calf lying in the sun near the bush.

OWEN

And nearer, nearer to the pens they go,
And the farmer riders draw the cattle near to the
ditch.
They drink, then draw on,
Towards the bidding cattle men who bid the
guineas.

OWEN

As they near the bidding men
They hear a grumbling man in the distance,
And there is a truck coming down the hill.
As the drone gets nearer, they drive them harder.

OWEN

As they hear the blaring sheep rolling along,
Boys are racing to see 'Old Thief' come along.
Sure enough 'Old Thief' is haggering last.
As they move nearer they move lazier.

OWEN

As they come towards the cruel shearing clippers,
The men sharpen up their cruel combs and cutters,
All ready to take off the sheep's clothes,
And wind them on the greasy table.

OWEN

212

As the greedy hawk hovers over the hill,
He carefully looks for sheep to eat;
He can see one now; down he goes to get it,
He takes a flap of his wings and flies away.

DAVID I.

The mist rushes in the gullies in the middle, like
     ghosts.
The wind comes drizzling it away.
The misting rain falls on the grooves of pine trees.
The drops fall from the needles like autumn leaves.

MARY

While the family dig the garden they talk.
The spades are like quarry picks on a hot day.
The people say it's hot and want to stop,
But adults say, 'Keep on digging'.

NELL

Swish, swish, the skim is going into the pigs' trough.
Swish, swish into the trough it goes.
The farmer comes and chases the big ones away.
Pigs and sows drink skim milk.

DAVID, 12 years

Away on yon hill, the loud dogs bark,
And closer a cow moves after its calf.
A car in the distance can be heard,
While people go about their usual work.

NELL

Bearded man, Dennis, 10 years

213

Godwits on the beach. Clifton. 10 years

'Hey, Boss! When are we going home?' they say,
Plonk, plonk! Men walk through the muddy
  swamp.
The turning on of the tap—swish—water.
'My word it's warm in this white tub.'
                              DAVID, 12 years

The people walk down to the sandy beach.
They walk on to the sugary sand with their lines.
The rocks are like people's faces staring.
The people sit and stare but not a word.
                              SARAH, 11 years

As the men crawl around the worm-picked rocks
Seagulls gather in lines and fly over the sea
That rolls like heavy brown earth,
And the big crayfish nip their way round the worm-
  picked rocks.
                              DAVID, 12 years

Around the rugged, ugly-looking rocks
A seagull's nest lies hidden amongst seaweeds,
And scrambling by them children play,
Nearly treading on the nest.
                              VALERIE

Nearly a year ago a house was left
By two people, who lived there for two years
And left it dying and sick with nothing to do.
No one to tread there and make a clatter with their
  shoes.
                              OWEN

No one to open the skleeky windows.
No one to open the rustling doors.
No one to prune the growing trees.
No one to feed the garden plants.
                              OWEN

214

All alone with nothing to say or do,
Nothing to listen to and no one to speak to,
Lying on sleepers and close to its death,
Dying in its sleep, farewelling its valley-sound
    friends
That sing a death song for its sleepy death.
                                                OWEN

As evening comes into the pretty valley
They see the mother sheep putting the lambs to
    sleep,
And as the evening swallows up the light
Men arrive home from their hard day's work.
                                                OWEN

Bang! A window shuts as it locks out the night.
Then in walks a weary man from hard work.
In comes the man to the mouth-watering food,
And the click, clack of dishes can be heard.
                                              VALERIE

Night comes just when the morepork cries.
The smelling of an old dead cow in the distance!
People feeding cows; the smelling of the hay!
Still, sounds can be heard as they walk up the path.
                                              ROSALIE

The dark is a blackbird flying across the sky,
Painting red paint across the horizon.

It turns the clouds into dancing flames
And blackens the sky for the stars to shine.
                                              DAVID I.

The moon creeps over the pitch black sky;
There are people talking in the houses.
Then the people hear the cry of the night bird
And flies buzzing around the walls of the room.
                                              CLIFTON

The morepork flies below the bluey sky
Flying frightened, spreading very fast;
Flying over trees and fences.
Slowing down, looking around for rats.
                                              MAVIS

Night comes when the blackbirds fly away
Back to Wekaroa, landing on sharp stones.
Then early in the morning they come back;
Mobs of blackbirds flying overhead.
                                              DAVID, 12 years

The moon tonight is a big rolling bag of gold
And from one corner of the room a bony rat creeps.
Then from the next room someone stirs
And from a bed someone starts to talk.
                                                TED

Bird on nest by Jenny

216

In the dark, all ghostly shadows move
They walk and take their shadows behind them.
Then all of a sudden the door bangs on top of their
    feet,
The handle moves with a shake and hides away the
    ghostly hand.

                                              NELL

As they go to bed at night they wonder what they
Are going to dream about.
As they go to sleep they hear the flames roaring
    loudly
And the sparkly wood sparkling louder and louder.

                                              OWEN

Lightning switches through the window at night,
When from the clouds the rumbling thunder comes.
Then from the beds the snore of people comes,
Which try to chase the night ghosts away.

                                              TED

The doors are locked, the houses are silent,
Now the darkness has gathered around the farms.
The sheep ghosts move slowly around the paddocks,
While chattering trees still talk on.

                                              NELL

The gates are shut on the braying cattle,
The doors are shut on the prowling men,
The henhouses are shut on the sleek rats,
And the night is silent for ever more.

                                              BRETT

The linocuts are reproduced from original prints made by the children.
Most photographs were taken by the author.
The book was designed by Roy Cowan.